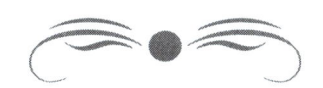

A PRACTICAL GUIDE TO

LEADERSHIP FOR LAWYERS

A PRACTICAL GUIDE TO
LEADERSHIP FOR LAWYERS

HERB RUBENSTEIN, J.D., MPA, DSS

INTRODUCTION BY
LARRY CENTER, J.D.
Director of Continuing Legal Education
Georgetown University, Washington, D.C.

NITA

NATIONAL INSTITUTE FOR TRIAL ADVOCACY

NITA Editorial Board

Thomas F. Geraghty, Chair
Northwestern University School of Law
Chicago, Illinois

Roxanne Barton Conlin
Roxanne Conlin & Associates
Des Moines, Iowa

Michael H. Ginsberg
Jones Day
Pittsburgh, Pennsylvania

Jo Ann Harris
Pace University School of Law
White Plains, New York

Michael A. Kelly
Walkup, Melodia, Kelly, Wecht & Schoenberger
San Francisco, California

Robert G. Krupka
Kirkland & Ellis
Los Angeles, California

Anthony J. Bocchino, NITA *Editor in Chief*
Temple University Beasley School of Law

Zelda Harris, NITA *Associate Editor*
University of Arizona College of Law

© 2005 by the National Institute for Trial Advocacy (NITA)

Printed in the United States of America. All rights reserved. These materials, or any parts or portions thereof, may not be reproduced in any form, written or mechanical, or be programmed into any electronic storage or retrieval system without the express written permission of the National Institute for Trial Advocacy unless such copying is expressly permitted by federal copyright law. Please direct inquiries to:

Reproduction Permission
National Institute for Trial Advocacy
53550 Generations Drive   (800) 225-6482   Fax (574) 271-8375
South Bend, IN 46635   E-mail: nita.1@nd.edu Web site: www.nita.org

Rubenstein, Herb, *A Practical Guide to Leadership for Lawyers*, (NITA, 2005).
11/05
ISBN 1-55681-949-8

Library of Congress Cataloging-in-Publication Data

Rubenstein, Herb, 1953-
    A Practical Guide to Leadership for Lawyers / by Herb Rubenstein ; introduction by Larry Center.
       p. cm.
       Includes bibliographical references and index.
       ISBN 1-55681-949-8 (alk. paper)
        1. Law—Study and teaching (Continuing education)—United States.
2. Lawyers—Training of—United States. 3. Leadership—Study and teaching (Continuing education)—United States. I. Title.

KF275.R82 2005

303.3'4'024340092--dc22

DEDICATION

This book is dedicated to all of those in the legal profession who have either already taken a leadership development course or who want to improve their leadership skills. The legal profession needs state supreme courts and bar associations to approve continuing legal education credit for leadership development courses. The time has come for our profession to take full advantage of the value that this emerging discipline can provide to one of the world's oldest professions. Larry Center, Director of the Continuing Legal Education Program of Georgetown University's Law Center, my alma mater, deserves special recognition for being one of the leaders promoting the goal of increasing leadership development training in the legal profession. His tireless work in editing this manuscript, his thoughtful introduction, and his constant inspiration throughout the effort that went into writing this book deserve special recognition and mention. He is truly a "leader of leaders" and a gift to the legal profession.

I also want to acknowledge Kathleen Rubenstein and George Gilbert for their work conducting research on leadership styles and organizing the brands of leadership section in the Appendix. This book would have never been written if not for the great support and encouragement of Terre Rushton, Associate Director for In-House Programs, of the National Institute for Trial Advocacy's National Education Center in Louisville, Colorado. I owe her a great debt. The leadership of Tony Bocchino at the National Institute for Trial Advocacy was also instrumental in this book breaking a 200-year barrier to bring leadership development education and strategies to the legal profession.

Finally, the chapter on Women, Leadership, and the Legal Profession is the result of the work and dedication of Laura Rothacker. I have learned immensely from her research, her perspective, and her leadership on this project.

TABLE OF CONTENTS

DEDICATION v

FOREWORD ix

AUTHOR'S PREFACE xiii

INTRODUCTION By Larry Center xv

CHAPTER ONE: The Benefits of Leadership Development for Lawyers . 1

CHAPTER TWO: Explaining Leadership: Theories, Practices, Styles, and Brands... 9

CHAPTER THREE: Leadership Behaviors and Motivation: Practical Approaches and Checklists 29

CHAPTER FOUR: The Ethics of Leadership 39

CHAPTER FIVE: Teaching Leadership Development in the Legal Profession: The New Model 47

CHAPTER SIX: Women, Leadership, and the Law............... 63

CHAPTER SEVEN: The Value of Leadership Development in the Profession 83

CHAPTER EIGHT: The Future of Leadership Education in the Legal Profession 103

APPENDIX A: Ninety Brands of Leadership Defined and Explained... 109

APPENDIX B: Leadership Education for Lawyers: Challenges and promise.. 139

BIBLIOGRAPHY 143

FOREWORD

One part of NITA's mission is to develop books, materials, and learning-by-doing programs designed to help lawyers develop the skills they will need for the 21st century. To that end it has developed books, materials, and learning-by-doing programs in addition to our trial, deposition, experts, and motion practice programs. NITA now has books, materials and programs in Supervisory Skills, Legal Strategy, Teaching Legal Strategy, and Advanced Negotiation and Mediation Theory and Practice. Is there really a need for a book, a set of materials and programming to teach leadership as a separate skill? Can leadership be taught?

The need is certainly there. The managing partner at a major New York firm recently remarked, "If a law firm such as ours cannot develop an ethos that we are about more than making money, then we simply can not keep the best and brightest at our firm. Frankly, our associates can make more money applying their considerable intellectual skills and talents in other areas than at a law firm. We need to create a learning organization that seeks to develop leaders and expert problem solvers, in the best sense of these words, if we will be able to provide a place where our associates and partners can find meaning and fulfillment."

More and more firms are taking on leadership training and development as part of their programs in professional development. Some hire psychologists to help them identify and assess leadership skills and strategies. Others have sent their senior associates to courses at Wharton. Other major firms have tried to develop leadership courses and curricula for their internal use.

What is true for the big firms is true for lawyers from all walks of practice and who work in all size firms. If a lawyer's aim is to simply make the most money, they can often do that in other ways than practice law. What makes the lawyer stay with the profession are the professional aspects of what she does, that is; to problem solve, offer wise advise, at times battle zealously, and at times be a peace maker, and strive to make a difference in the lives of her clients to the end that justice is served, and society is better off for it.

NITA has learned of the need for leadership skills while teaching the other skills course it teaches. While teaching Supervisory Skills, NITA been asked for help in understanding the difference between supervising, mentoring and leadership. Lawyers in these courses are hungry for information about how to develop "ownership" over work, maturity in judgment that looks at the big picture as well and the immediate task, and teaches supervisees how to exercise good judgment, and give wise, considered advice. While teaching Legal Strategy, we've been asked to explain how best to develop an effective approach to strategic decision making that produces not only excellent client service, but a shared language of the best ethical decision making. We've discussed how to measure litigation strategy against leadership principles: peace first, lowest cost, simplest to execute, least public exposure. While teaching our Advanced Negotiation and Mediation programs, we've been asked to teach how to resist becoming over wedded to your case, avoid losing by winning, how to develop techniques to keep from becoming angry and reactive. There is a hunger in these courses for discussions and understanding of the "stuff of leadership" of leading from a strong sense of self and priorities, of maturity, of how to develop a shared language of mission, of leading—but as partners, and leading from behind, not from ahead or on top of junior employees.

Herb Rubenstein has shown up just in time to help NITA in its development of books, materials and learning-by-doing programs for teaching leadership. His book describes for the lawyers the history and development of different leadership models for effective leadership. It provides a test for measuring leadership, and exploring different styles and strategies for developing "ownership" of work, a focus on excellent client service, a share language of purpose and mission, and ways to insure that firm priorities are in order and are followed. He recommends the development and use of simulations and role playing that place students into situations that require leadership skills. He then recommends that teachers provide feedback and facilitate discussion of approaches and skills that can lead to "repeatable" behaviors of excellent leadership.

Herb's book is an important step in NITA's process of developing materials and programs from training leaders in the law. It provides the profession with a much needed bridge into the language of leadership, and a way of initiating an important dialogue about what matters most in the practice of law.

Paul J. Zwier
Director of Education, National Institute for Trial Advocacy
Professor of Law, Emory University School of Law

AUTHOR'S PREFACE

The field of leadership development, which has expanded rapidly over the past forty years, has made few inroads into the classical education of law students or in continuing legal education courses. This book is about how that is changing rapidly with major law firms hiring Wharton, Harvard, and leadership development trainers and consultants to teach members of their firms leadership development theory, skills, and practices. The field of law now requires greater leadership development skills among its practitioners and managers of law firms than ever before.

As an attorney who has been a member of the Board of Directors of the International Leadership Association and co-chair of its national conference in 2004, I have a unique perspective on how the legal profession can benefit, and how continuing legal education administrators can also benefit, from the intersection of the two disciplines of law and leadership development. Both professions, law and the leadership development industry, would benefit greatly from the development of a broad range of leadership development courses designed specifically for lawyers and law students. This book is a beginning in the evolution of leadership development for lawyers and is aimed at both the individual legal practitioner, and government, non-profit, in-house attorneys, and law firms of all sizes.

Appendix A to this book explains approximately ninety brands of leadership currently on the market. You may find your leadership style and be able to identify the leadership style of others. More importantly, this appendix is provided so you will have instant access to a summary of the leadership development literature that may help guide you in finding and developing the leadership approach that is best for you and best for situations you and your legal organization face on a regular basis.

INTRODUCTION

Leadership has become a popular subject in the past several years. All one needs to do is peruse the management section in any bookstore to confirm that fact. In fact, one might argue that "leadership" has replaced TQM as the manager's self-help mantra of this century's first decade. The proliferation of leadership books and articles might have the unintended consequence of convincing some managers that leadership is merely the latest fad, soon to be replaced by another "flavor of the month" in the annals of management literature.

Drawing such a conclusion would not only be foolish, but dangerous for the future of organizations. Every organization, large or small, needs excellent leadership. Whether we consider one of the Fortune 100 multinational corporations or a local non-profit charitable organization, all organizations will benefit from wise, enlightened and visionary leadership.

Unfortunately, most people who become leaders have not benefited from a formal education in leadership. Leadership is not a common major within our colleges and universities. Even at our best business schools, leadership has rarely been a significant part of the curriculum. The majority of leaders in the corporate, academic, not-for-profit and professional spheres have learned leadership skills the hard way: through experience, through mistakes and, if they are fortunate, from mentors with years of leadership experience.

My interest in the leadership field grew from my first exposure to Stephen Covey's *The Seven Habits of Highly Effective People*, now the best-selling business book ever published. After reading that book, I decided to become a licensed facilitator of the workshop based upon it. For the past eight years, I have facilitated these workshops for employees at my parent institution, Georgetown University, and have delivered many lectures and workshops based upon this material for organizations and associations across the United States.

This in turn produced a greater interest in the entire field of leadership, and as I immersed myself in the readings of leadership pioneers from Robert Greenleaf to Warren Bennis to Peter Senge, I began to wonder why this leadership revolution has not made its way into my profession, the legal profession.

For the past twenty-five years, I have been involved in the continuing legal education industry. Since 1985, I have served as the head of a continuing legal education (CLE) department at Georgetown University Law Center in Washington, DC. During these past twenty years, I have served as a leader and active member of the Association for Continuing Legal Education, the international organization representing the CLE industry. As a part of my job during this span of more than two decades, I have followed closely the trends within the legal profession.

The practice of law in 2005 is far different than it was twenty years ago. The collegiality that characterized law firms of the 1980's is missing from many law firms today. The emphasis on the bottom line has dramatically increased. Whereas law firms used to wait for clients to walk through the front door or depend on several big rain-makers, today more and more law firms are hiring chief marketing officers. Firms are even training their lawyers in sales skills, once a foreign word for law firms. Firms are also hiring chief operating officers or chief business officers, adopting the corporate model utilized by many of their brethren in the private sector.

One would think that in this era of emphasis on the bottom line, on business practices and on client development, law firms would have fully embraced leadership as an essential tool for today's legal leaders. After all, excellent leadership would help a law firm become more efficient, attract more clients, retain its top lawyers and staff members and grow more profitable. Nevertheless, law firms have not devoted dollars and time to teaching their managing partners, practice group heads, senior partners and senior associates about leadership. Why, in this decade of rapid change in law firm practice when corporations are devoting so many resources to leadership training, have law firms dragged their feet on leadership development?

Traditionally, corporations have been years ahead of law firms in adopting training techniques and mandating training for all employees. Whether one considers the benefits of distance learning or the widespread adoption of on-line education, corporations have been training employees around the world for many years. Only recently have law firms and other legal organizations begun considering and implementing such programs.

Law firms have eschewed training in what many consider "soft skills" for decades. Traditional continuing legal education has focused upon substantive law developments or the improvement of identified, more technical, legal skills. Continuing legal education providers who have offered courses in management or leadership skills for lawyers have encountered difficulties in getting these courses accredited for Mandatory Continuing Legal Education credit or have seen these courses suffer from very low attendance. Even in-house training courses in management and leadership have been rare.

The lack of these courses is ironic because law firm leaders are generically smart, with years of formal education and years of experience in the work place. Intellectually, they know that a successful law firm must be based upon great leadership. They know that such leadership must include a commitment to hiring the right people, lawyers and non-lawyers, putting them in the proper jobs and then "growing" these people as they progress through their careers.

Legal leaders who wish to grow their people have to start with a positive attitude. They must look for the best in people. They must see people's potential. They need to believe that all persons who work for them, including attorneys and non-attorneys, can be more than they were when they started their jobs. They must be fair, but tough. They have to hold people accountable and not settle for any less than people being at their best. In order to be leaders who create other leaders, they must stretch their employees, put them in uncomfortable positions, positions that force them to face new problems and develop new solutions. They must persuade their people that they can establish ambitious goals and meet them and that they have exciting professional futures.

Too often, law firms focus only on people's professional lives. Yet if they are to truly coach people successfully and develop leaders, they must pay significant attention to their personal lives as well. They must focus on their competence and their character, making sincere investments of time in their people. Getting to know colleagues as people and not just as workers can pay huge dividends for leaders in legal organizations. If people know that their leaders care for them as human beings, that leaders are respectful of their strengths and understanding of their weaknesses, that their leaders are always striving to put them in the best possible light in front of their peers and others, they will be willing to go the extra mile when it becomes necessary. And when they become leaders later in their careers, they will demonstrate the same behavior with their peers and colleagues.

Excellent leaders at law firms know what motivates their people. Like a coach or manager of a sports team, they must balance egos and needs. They must know who is motivated by a pat on the back and who is motivated by a push. All of us who have read management literature know the gurus maintain that most people are not motivated only by money. Money can be important, but equally important are praise, recognition, the opportunity to develop new skills, the chance to acquire new knowledge, the promise of advancement within the organization and the chance to contribute as part of a team to the process and outcomes of the firm and clients.

At the same time they motivate people, great legal leaders encourage lawyers and non-lawyers to develop their skills, skills that further their career aspirations while serving the firm, clients, and the profession. Simultaneously, successful leaders in legal organizations help people develop knowledge, knowledge about their jobs, about their clients, about the firm and about the role they play at the firm. Great leaders do not stop at helping people identify the skills and knowledge they wish to gain. They also assist them in identifying the relationships they need to build. They realize that effective human relationships are the underpinning of professional success for everyone in the legal profession.

Great leaders know that they must develop other people. To do so, they must serve as role models. In fact, they serve in this capacity, whether they like it or not. They act as role models by design and by default, through acts of omission and acts of commission. Every moment of the day they are serving as role models and they know that people pay much more attention to what they do than what they say. They know that talking about honesty and integrity within the office does no good if they do not act with honesty and integrity on a consistent basis. The best legal leaders know that if they have acted in a fashion contrary to their principles, the most important action they can take is to apologize sincerely to the people affected. Many leaders and colleagues at law firms are possessed of huge egos. These egos prevent them from apologizing to their peers or staffs after they have erred, treated someone unfairly or not followed up on a commitment. Excellent leaders know there is no surer way to lose the trust of people than to ignore errors and not apologize. Apologizing sincerely shows people that leaders are fallible just like them. It shows people that leaders will tolerate mistakes and that they should not be afraid of making them. It reveals a leader's humanity and humility. In effect, it makes people stronger leaders.

The fact that people pay more attention to what we do than what we say is known by many effective leaders. However, a less-frequently cited phrase is "People pay more attention to who you are than what you do." This means that people watch leaders, in law firms and elsewhere, every second. While people judge us by what we do and what we say, in the larger picture, people judge us by the kind of person we are. How do we carry and project ourselves? How do we respond to crises? How do we deal with the unexpected? How do we handle success and failure? Do we learn from our mistakes? Do we praise people publicly and criticize people privately? Are we consistent in the manner in which we treat people? Do we treat people equally, regardless of their race, age, title or salary levels? Are we people they perceive as trustworthy? Do we listen carefully when others speak, especially when they are expressing an alternate viewpoint?

If law firm leaders remember at all times that they are role models, they can have an enormous impact upon the people they coach and with whom they work. The future leaders on their teams will remember the behaviors they modeled many years later.

True leaders know that one of the most important skills they can teach the people on their teams is the ability to coach and lead themselves. Encouraging people to build their own leadership muscles is much more difficult than it sounds, especially for leaders who are used to micromanaging others and being in total control. Empowering others means in essence ceding control by trusting others to do as good a job as they can do. Unless leaders are willing to surrender some control as they coach and mentor them, these people will never be able to develop to their fullest potential. The best leaders realize that helping people reach their fullest potential is one of their most critical roles.

How can law firm leaders and leaders in other types of legal organizations that comprise the legal profession grow to appreciate all these qualities of excellent leaders? How can the leadership revolution that has impacted businesses throughout the world impact the legal profession? How can Mandatory Legal Education boards gain sufficient insight to start granting CLE credit for leadership courses?

This important process will not occur overnight. It will take place gradually, one step at a time. Law firm leaders and leaders of other types of legal organizations in the profession must be educated about leadership principles, about the evolution of leadership knowledge in this country and its value for organizations. They must see the positive effect of leadership training at peer law firms and within legal agencies. Slowly this process is starting to take place. Two years ago the national law firm Reed Smith, LLP started Reed Smith University in conjunction with the Wharton School of Business at the University of Pennsylvania. A significant part of the curriculum is leadership. This year the international law firm DLA Piper Rudnick, LLP signed a contract with the Harvard Business School to teach leadership and management skills to its firm leaders.

Much more is needed. A paradigm shift must take place. Fortunately, books like this one will help lead the way. In this important work, Herb Rubenstein shows lawyers WHY leadership is so vital for every successful legal organization in the twenty-first century. He takes the reader on a guided tour of the leadership literature of the past fifty years. He identifies the various brands of leadership that authors and business leaders have been teaching and practicing, pointing out the strengths and weaknesses of each. He shares success stories of leaders who have used their leadership skills in order to lead their firms and companies to new heights. Finally, Herb introduces the reader to the critical concept of "leaders of leaders," people who can significantly impact the legal profession for decades to come.

I invite you to take this leadership journey with Herb as your guide. It will enlighten you, educate you and inspire you. Most important, it will change you.

Lawrence J. Center

November, 2005

CHAPTER ONE
THE BENEFITS OF LEADERSHIP DEVELOPMENT FOR LAWYERS

Lawyers are called upon to lead every day. Although the lawyer is the "agent" and the client is the "principal," lawyers have a duty to lead their clients through providing accurate technical advice, principled counseling, and a rigorous evaluation of the client's situation, goals, and resources and those of the adversary. This is the first book on leadership designed specifically for lawyers and written by a lawyer. It is intended to answer a question that is growing in the field of law.

U.S. Judge James Barr frames this question thoughtfully and cogently:

> I am delving into whether there is support for the hypothesis that leadership skills developed and implemented by individual lawyers (even when not serving in bar organizations) can significantly impact and influence an entire legal community in such areas as (1) improved ethical and civility standards and performance, (2) more effective assimilation of new lawyers into the legal community, and (3) improved relations between bench and bar. In other words, I am at least curious about whether development of leadership skills by individual lawyers can positively impact the quality of lawyering in a legal community—even when working outside the institutional (i.e., bar organization) context.

This book is the first systematic attempt to answer Judge Barr's question. Only time will tell whether the answer is affirmative for all or most lawyers. But the thesis of this book is that when lawyers begin to understand the basic theories of leadership as developed over the millennia and enhanced in the leadership literature over the past fifty years, and when lawyers begin to understand some of the many brands of leadership on the market today, lawyers will be able to improve their skills and aptitude as leaders; to provide better legal services; to create better law firms; to improve the associations, foundations, and organizations that support and are supported by the legal profession; and they will improve both the reputation of lawyers and the legal profession as a whole. Accomplishing each of these goals is a tall task in and of itself. Expecting that a new emphasis on leadership training will help transform and improve an entire profession certainly can be described as a "stretch goal." It is this stretch goal that serves as the basis of this book.

This book is based on the author's work as a lawyer for more than twenty years, as a trial attorney handling matters for plaintiffs as well as defendants, who has practiced in hundreds of courtrooms and argued and settled cases in many jurisdictions. In addition, this author has been an adjunct professor of leadership, entrepreneurship, strategic planning, and ethics at five universities, has reviewed a substantial part of the leadership literature, and has been a member of the Board of Directors of the International Leadership Association and served as its international conference co-chair. Most importantly, this author has been hired by many clients not just to be a good technical lawyer, but to exercise leadership in resolving difficult challenges faced by clients and the opposing side.

This firsthand experience of knowing the leadership development literature, and using the skills, training, and leadership education that I have had the privilege to receive has contributed to successes for clients that could not have been achieved through using only the skills and analytical techniques taught in law schools. Leadership education has evolved to the point where almost all professions are starting to reap significant rewards from taking leadership courses. Becoming familiar with leadership theory, and pursuing leadership courses and training help people create their own leadership styles. This book designed specifically for lawyers and non-lawyers who work in the legal profession will help you get in touch with your own leadership approach, and give you practice and guidance in being a more effective leader.

THE BENEFITS OF LEADERSHIP DEVELOPMENT FOR LAWYERS

The general public—and clients—look to lawyers to be leaders. They expect lawyers to be leaders first because they know the law. But such knowledge is only a small part of being a leader. Research by Daniel Goleman on emotional intelligence has revealed that one's ability to manage one's emotional responses and the emotional responses of others is critical to leaders today. Research and previous publications by this author show that leaders know how to "manage conversations, not dominate them." Second, lawyers are often called upon to serve as members of boards of directors, boards of advisors, and boards of trustees; to conduct high-level investigations into wrongdoing; to uncover corruption; to make high-stakes presentations to opposing counsel, government agencies, trial courts, and arbitration panels; to interact intelligently and cogently with the media; and to negotiate successfully regarding matters that can make or break the financial, emotional, and institutional lives and reputations of clients. The level of leadership required in each of these activities is extraordinary, yet the legal profession during the past ten years has given continuing legal education (CLE) credit for courses such as "Creating PowerPoint Presentations," but not for courses to help lawyers become better leaders.

This book is designed to help lawyers be better leaders, and to help change the legal profession for the better as well. By guiding lawyers through the leadership literature in a manner they can understand, by using examples of lawyers being leaders that are applicable to the everyday lives of lawyers throughout the United States, and by drawing on the experience of many lawyers who have worked all of their lives on their leadership skills, this book is designed to help a lawyer objectively evaluate how good a leader the lawyer is today while creating the beginning of a path to assist the lawyer in becoming a better leader in the future.

This book is written so that the basic tenets of leadership that will be learned by readers can be applied in client-oriented settings, in law firms, and other organizational contexts where lawyers have responsibilities for leading and managing enterprises. This book is written for all lawyers, regardless of their particular jobs, employers, or practice expertise. It is unrealistic to think that law schools will start offering classes on leadership because in three years (or four years for night students) law schools have to teach so much information to students to just prepare them to pass bar exams and understand and appreciate the technical demands of practicing law.

One law school, Harvard, offers a course taught by Philip Heymann called "Leadership in the Public Sector." Professor Heymann has recommended to this author that every law school teach at least one course in leadership. At present, the learning of leadership knowledge and skills is left up to those lawyers who take courses outside the legal profession, are self-taught, or learn from a mentor in their organization. This book and the courses on leadership for lawyers to be taught by the National Institute for Trial Advocacy (NITA), the Office of Personnel Management of the U.S. Government, and by others represent an important opening for lawyers to a new world of leadership theories and practical suggestions regarding how to be a better leader, and thereby, be a better lawyer.

There are starting to be significant developments in the teaching of leadership for lawyers. The Cincinnati Bar Association has conducted a leadership for lawyers course for some time. The Alabama Supreme Court has instituted a leadership program for lawyers. The Business Law Institute of the Colorado Bar Association has created a leadership seminar taught by this author with CLE credit approved for this course. The American Psychological Association recently published, *Lawyer Know Thyself*, a book that discusses personality strengths and weaknesses with a view toward assisting lawyers in becoming better leaders.[1] Courses in "professionalism" and "ethics" touch on leadership behaviors and values. State and local bar associations and the American Bar Association hold leadership classes designed to help lawyers become better leaders within those organizations. The Oregon Bar Association has a leadership development program for new lawyers. The Renaissance Lawyer Society promotes stronger leadership development among lawyers to help address some of the challenges that are currently affecting the legal profession.

---

[1] *Lawyer Know Thyself* (Susan Swaim Daicoff: American Psychological Association, 2004).

The problems and challenges that currently beset the legal profession are well known within the industry but not deeply understood by most lawyers, their clients, or law schools. These problems as suggested by this author's review of books and articles in the field, include the following:

- High rate of dissatisfaction among young attorneys
- Poor reputation of lawyers within the society
- High departure rate for trained, qualified, and certified lawyers from the legal profession
- Growing economic pressures on law firms of all sizes, especially large firms
- High levels of client dissatisfaction and formal complaints and malpractice actions against lawyers
- Growing levels of associate turnover
- Prevalence of outdated governance practices at many law firms
- Continuing evidence of a glass ceiling for women in law firms
- Client challenges to paying increasingly large legal bills and insistence on alternative billing structures
- Growing numbers of ethical complaints against lawyers
- Increasing competition and growing use of questionable means to obtain clients/business
- Increasing lack of civility among lawyers
- Increasing delays in litigation, arbitration, and even mediation
- Lack of training in leadership in a profession whose members lead clients, lead organizations, serve on boards of directors, and hold high political and governmental positions, all without the benefit of the knowledge created in the field of leadership development during the past fifty years

These challenges dominate discussions at bar association conferences. Improving the leadership skills of those in the legal profession can, to some extent, help address some, if not all, of these challenges that lawyers confront.

The legal industry is one of the most rapidly evolving professions in the world. From 1950 to 2005 the legal profession has grown rapidly. During this time frame, record numbers of law graduates, record numbers of practicing attorneys, record numbers of women entering the profession, record salaries for private practitioners, record numbers of large jury verdicts and increasingly large average jury verdicts, have propelled the legal profession to stay busy, self-confident, and self-assured.

Today the legal profession is beset by competitive pressures from technology that put the law, statutes, court decisions, and legal procedures at the fingertips of anyone who can use the Internet. Clients can perform more of their own work if they so choose. In-house legal counsel, whose corporate employers have the capital to spend on large legal staffs and technology, have taken back significant amounts of work from private law firms. Lawyers now often advertise and attract clients based on the quality of their advertising rather than on the quality of their abilities as lawyers. Mergers of law firms, unheard of just twenty years ago, are moving forward at a fever pitch, combining law firms with over 1,000 employees. These financial and industry statistics all point to societal and economic pressures that will challenge every aspect of the legal profession economically and organizationally.

Today leadership development is essential not only for those who lead these megafirms, but also for sole practitioners and lawyers in small firms who rely on their leadership contributions in their communities as a significant element of their business development and reputation-enhancing activities. In addition, in-house counsel are more and more expected to participate intelligently at the corporate strategy table. Thus, leadership development has become a critical component of their needed skill set as well.

The Sarbanes-Oxley Act has placed those lawyers who investigate and counsel corporations on white-collar criminal activities, whistle blowing, accounting, governance, and reporting issues in

THE BENEFITS OF LEADERSHIP DEVELOPMENT FOR LAWYERS

the position of having to be "leaders of leaders," a term that will be extensively discussed in this book. As the Sarbanes-Oxley principles are extended to the nonprofit world, academic institutions, unions, and eventually governmental organizations at all levels, lawyers' (and auditors') leadership skills will be in great demand. Lawyers will be expected to be not only the ones who tell organizations what to do, but also will be required to help lead these client organizations into a brave new world. This new world will include creating significant governance oversight, financial oversight, internal fiscal controls, accurate financial reporting, and disclosing adverse material financial information to investors and the general public sooner rather than later. Lawyers in the twenty-first century will be more involved in leading the client organizations they serve than ever before.

The legal profession is already struggling mightily with new and subtle changes to the attorney-client privilege, propelled by lawyers' knowing about fraudulent financial activities of their clients. The new role of independent directors who demand that the company's lawyers tell them what they know, which previously would have been attorney-client privileged and never told to these "outsiders," is helping lawyers gain a deeper understanding of what it means to be a leader in a disclosure-rich world.

These developments in the legal profession strongly suggest that lawyers should seek and the legal profession should offer excellent leadership development education and training to all members of our profession and the non-lawyer employees with whom they work. This book is a start. Many lawyers will use it to begin their quest to become better leaders. Many lawyers will use it to add to their many hours spent becoming a self-taught leader. And law firms, professional legal organizations, law students, and those who are considering going to law school will use leadership development training to achieve a competitive advantage over other law firms, law students, and fellow lawyers who do not seek to improve their leadership skills on a regular basis.

Finally, after reading this book, the reader might consider taking one of the many "leadership assessment" questionnaires now available. It is beyond the scope of this book to analyze these inventories or to recommend any one of them. This book will serve as a guide to learning about the leadership development literature, successful leadership behaviors, and how lawyers can use their newly enhanced leadership skills to improve their lawyering and management abilities. Moreover, it will also serve as a guide to lawyers who seek to learn more about their own leadership styles and approaches.

Chapter 2 provides a review of the major theories of leadership and those leadership behaviors that have withstood the tests of time.

CHAPTER TWO
EXPLAINING LEADERSHIP: THEORIES, PRACTICES, STYLES, AND BRANDS

Leadership is the mobilization of the followers.
James MacGregor Burns

What is leadership? *Leadership is the creation and fulfillment of worthwhile opportunities by honorable means.*

There are over three hundred definitions of leadership today. There are thousands of books on leadership, ten generally accepted theories of leadership, and several theories regarding motivation, an important subset of leadership. This chapter is a shortcut for lawyers, law students, and those who work in the legal profession, through the leadership literature.

One basic notion of leadership defines it as *"problem solving."* Leaders are people who solve problems and often people who see problems and understand them first. This simplified notion of leadership, problem solving, describes much of what leaders do. Certainly leaders must spot or identify problems early enough so that a solution that is not too costly can be fashioned to solve the problem. Although leadership will always be about solving problems, there is a new branch of leadership supported and fostered by this book that is not just about solving problems. Rather, it is about creating platforms and standards that people and societies are to follow. The people who undertake this task are what I call "leaders of leaders," and they will be discussed at the end of this chapter. Lawyers and the legal profession are uniquely situated in American society to perform this critical role of being "leaders of leaders."

LEADERSHIP FOR LAWYERS

The following are some of the "brands of leadership" on the market today.

Assigned Leadership	Executive Development
Connective Leadership	Team Building
Balanced Leadership	Coaching
Muscular Leadership	Situational Leadership
Toxic Leadership	Principle-Centered Leadership
Fusion Leadership	
Complexity Leadership	Values-Centered Leadership
Character Based Leadership	Inclusive Leadership
Emergent Leadership	Servant Leadership
Directive Leadership	Transactional Leadership
Participative Leadership	Transformational Leadership
Ethical Leadership	Enlightened Leadership
Principled Leadership	Leadership at Every Step
Team Leadership	Leading Change
Achievement-Oriented Leadership	Values-Based Leadership
	Continuous Leadership
Supportive Leadership	Rational Leadership
Charismatic Leadership	Visionary Leadership
Wholehearted Leadership	Strategic Leadership
Level 5 Leadership	Virtual Leadership
Authentic Leadership	Inspired Leadership
Leadership Development	Leaders Building Leaders
Leadership Training	Leading Upward

EXPLAINING LEADERSHIP: THEORIES, PRACTICES, STYLES, AND BRANDS

Tomorrow Leader	Collaborative Leadership
Quantum Leadership	Appreciative Leadership
Alpha Leadership	Leadership as a Process
Lead by Design	Proactive Leadership
Results-Based Leadership	Generative Leadership
Trickle-Up Leadership	Revolutionary Leadership
Leaders to Leaders	Unnatural Leadership
Formative Leadership	Empowering Leadership
Distributive Leadership	Leadership by Example
Integral Leadership	Functional Leadership
Cross-Border Leadership	Organizational Leadership
Invisible Leadership	Operational Leadership
Social Leadership	Innovative Leadership
Contributory Leadership	Creative Leadership
Conscious Leadership	Synergistic Leadership
Transcendent Leadership	Entrepreneurial Leadership
Integrated Leadership	Steward Leadership
Institutionalized Leadership	Military Leadership

Each one of these "brands" is described in Appendix A. There are probably hundreds, if not thousands, of brands of leadership that are not mentioned above. Regardless of how many brands of soap there are on the market, the basic concept of soap is not very hard to figure out. Each one of these brands of leadership is a particular approach toward solving some type of problem or creating some set of standards or platforms designed to guide future behavior.

There are ten specific theories of leadership, but no general theory of leadership. Each of these theories tries to explain how leaders become leaders or how leaders work when they are leading people. The first nine theories are based on Northouse's work, and are presented in an "evolutionary" order. Each theory builds on the previous theory. The tenth theory is a contribution to the leadership literature by this author, and dates back to Jethro in the Book of Exodus. The ten theories are as follows:

1. The Trait Theory: People with certain favorable physical, mental, personality, and emotional traits are more likely, if not destined, to be leaders.

2. The Style Approach: Leadership is a function of the style of behavior a person brings to a situation. Typical styles of leadership activity include Team Management, Authority-Compliance, Country Club Management, and Impoverished Management.

3. The Situational Approach: Leaders must "read" a situation accurately and determine what combination of supportive and directive behaviors is appropriate to achieve the goal of the leader. This leadership theory suggests that leaders adapt their styles and behavior based on understanding the full content and context of the situation in which they are operating, their role, the goals of the situation, and the resources they have to use and direct.

4. The Contingency Theory: Understanding and developing successful leadership behaviors is based on analyzing three key factors: leader-member relations, task structure, and position power. Contingency theory shows how the success of certain styles of leadership is contingent on the circumstances in which they are used. Thus, this theory suggests that the relationship between the leaders and the followers should have a strong impact on the leader and the appropriate leadership style that will be effective in that situation.

5. Path-Goal Theory: This is the motivational theory of leadership. This theory suggests that a major goal of leadership is to stimulate performance and satisfaction among those led by the leader. Under this theory the classic behaviors of the leader are (1) to identify goals and to secure "buy in," support, enthusiasm, ownership of these goals by followers; (2) to identify all key obstacles and barriers to achieving the goals; (3) ensure proper training and resources for followers in their effort to achieve goals; (4) to organize and direct the actions of the followers in their efforts to achieve goals; (5) to monitor all activity and guide any changes in strategy, resources, and actions necessary to achieve goals; (6) to identify precisely and accurately when the goal is achieved or the shortcomings that result from the effort; (7) to acknowledge and reward systematically all followers for contributions in the effort to achieve the goals; and (8) to set new goals and expectations for the group and repeat the process.

6. Leader-Member Exchange Theory: Leadership is a function of a relationship in which followers give to a leader leadership status and responsibilities and leaders accept that status and perform leadership acts that the followers accept. The relationship between the leader and followers is one of partnership rather than control. Power is equally shared by members with the leader, and the leader's ability and authority to lead is always a function of the support he or she has from the members.

7. Transformational Leadership: Leadership is a process where leaders and followers work together in a manner that changes and transforms individuals and groups. It is a dynamic process that assesses the followers' needs and motives and seeks the input of the followers at each critical stage in the leadership process. Transformational leadership presupposes that the goal of the leader is to promote change and improvement for the betterment and with the assistance of the followers. This type of leadership has an explicit goal turning followers into future leaders.

8. Team Leadership: This theory assumes that all leaders are leaders of teams and the major functions of a leader are (1) to help the group determine which goals and tasks it wants to achieve; (2) to help create enabling processes and direct the group so that it achieves the goals and tasks; (3) to keep the group (and the leader) supplied with the right resources, training, and supplies; (4) to set standards for behavior, success, and ethics; (5) to diagnose and remedy group deficiencies; (6) to forecast impending environmental changes to help inform and steer the group appropriately;

and (7) to help maintain and defend the group by organizing it and ensuring its proper internal functioning.

9. Psychodynamic Approach: Leadership requires that leaders understand their own psychological makeup and the psychological makeup of those they lead. Leaders using this theory are those who understand (1) the followers' attitudes, potential, behaviors, and expected responses to leadership; (2) the level of maturity of followers and its impact on their responses to leadership actions; (3) the desires and motivational keys of followers; (4) the meaning and interpretation by followers of language, behavior, symbols, and situations; (5) the proper balance of dependence and independence appropriate for a given group of followers; (6) the proper psychological relationship between the leader and followers; and (7) of the psychodynamic interplay between the leader and followers and between and among leaders as well.

10. Leaders of Leaders: This theoretical construct states that the job of a leader of followers is completely different from that of a leader of leaders. Leaders of followers are mainly "problem solvers." Leaders of leaders establish platforms and seek to create an environment so that followers can act as leaders themselves, solve their own "problems," and make excellent decisions consistent with the platform that the leader of leaders sets. In addition, the leaders of leaders concept incorporates the idea that the platform set by the leader of leaders will improve over time because the followers and other leaders will be encouraged to test the platform in the real world, find deficiencies, and report proposed improvements for the platform to the leader of leaders. The major role of the leader of leaders is to create this platform and not to make decisions in particular situations. This job is delegated to the leaders whom the leader of leaders leads.

We expand this section on leaders of leaders because it is the leadership theory that fits most closely with the real world of lawyers and those in the legal profession. First, the legal profession serves clients. Second, it is the clients' lawful goals that the legal professional is designed to help achieve.

Our law firm's work with companies, educational institutions, government agencies, the courts, and nonprofit organizations over the past two decades has revealed that there is an important, even critical distinction between being a leader of followers and being a leader of leaders that is relevant to the legal profession. The skills, competencies, aptitudes, values, decision-making approaches, strengths, daily roles, and job descriptions are radically different for these two separate categories of leaders.

Just as Warren Bennis defined the differences between leaders and managers (*On Becoming a Leader*), this book spells out for the legal profession how lawyers can become better lawyers and law firms can become better law firms by adopting the basic tenets of the leader of leaders approach to leadership. I will use three examples of people who clearly fit into the category of leaders of leaders. Many other examples exist both today and historically. In order to introduce what I mean by leaders of leaders, it is important to give a working definition of what a leader does and what a leader of leaders does.

A Leader of Followers Is a Person or Group of People Who:

> 1. Identifies a significant gap between what exists today and an improved state that can be created in the future (Vision)
>
> 2. Understands enough about why the current situation exists to know which resources to gather and what forces to apply to solve the problems of the current situation (Grounding)
>
> 3. Identifies and communicates a clear, achievable, and understandable path toward improving the current situation (Direction)
>
> 4. Identifies the exact combination of resources (capital, people, innovation, techniques, etc.) needed to bring about the desired result (Feasibility Planning)
>
> 5. Builds the organizational capacity to achieve the desired result (Developer)

6. Gathers and organizes resources taking into account economics, logistics, legal, and other requirements necessary to deploy these resources successfully (Enrollment and Collaboration)

7. Oversees the project and management plan (including budget) ensuring that the resources used are gathered and deployed in the optimal order and amount (Efficiency)

8. Achieves through leadership an improvement that people can see and identify with that is consistent with the vision or desired outcome (Success)

9. Rewards the people (salary, acknowledgement, etc.), the capital (profit or staying within budget), and all resources associated with the project so that followers would want to work with that leader again (Caretaker)

10. Identifies a new gap between a current situation and a desired outcome (Vision)

This is what a leader of followers does. Essentially, the ten steps listed above are ten steps in solving a problem. Leaders of leaders act differently. They do not do the things listed above when they are acting as leaders of leaders. The section below identifies what leaders of leaders do.

A Leader of Leaders Is a Person or Group of People Who:

1. Sees a series or class of problems or gaps between the current situation and a desired state of affairs (Broad Vision)

2. Identifies and develops workable solutions to sets of current problems by developing rules, principles, ways of thinking, innovations, and responses that address classes of problems (Systems Solutions)

3. Creates one or more platforms by writing, speaking, and effectively communicating his or her innovations and solutions so that other leaders can use these platforms to address classes of problems (Platform Builder)

4. Creates a communication structure that gets the leader of leaders' message out to leaders and followers in a consistent and reliable manner (Manages the Conversation)

5. Creates a relationship with the leaders they lead so they adopt the leader of leaders' platform and begin using the new solutions and innovations to address the classes of problems (Enrollment)

6. Creates a communication system that ensures that the leader of leaders gets regular, systematic feedback from the leaders they lead as well as their followers regarding the platform including information to inform the leader of leaders as to what works and does not work regarding the leader of leaders' platform (Builds and Feeds the Feedback System)

7. Uses this feedback to improve the platform, the solutions, the principles, and the rules of the leader of leaders so that the future platforms, writings, and teachings become a better foundation that leaders and followers can use and turn to for answers and guidance (Constant Improvement)

8. Monitors how leaders and followers are applying the platform, teachings and innovations to ensure that the use is both widespread and consistent with the leader of leaders' vision and ideas about how to achieve improvements (Overseer)

9. Takes decisive action when the platform is misused to prevent future problems (Guardian)

10. Identifies a new class of problems to solve and develops new platforms and expands current platforms to address this new class of problems (Broad Vision)

The Distinction Between a Leader and a Leader of Leaders

The platform created by the leader of leaders lets the law firm, legal organization, or other entities know how that leader would respond to a given situation. Leaders of leaders make sure that their platform is well known, understood, and followed by those they lead. Therefore, when a situation arises and a leader or follower looks for guidance, that leader or follower looks to the leader of leaders' platform, teachings, writings, speeches, solutions, innovations, guidance, principles, and positions in order to figure out how that leader of leaders would have wanted that leader or follower to respond to improve the situation at hand and the world at large.

Today leaders of leaders can lead thousands of leaders who, in turn, use the leaders of leaders' platform to lead millions of followers. No leader of leaders can respond to the millions of questions that leaders and followers could ask in response to specific situations. Therefore, developing and communicating the platform, the set of rules, principles, solutions, innovations, examples, and ideas in writing or in some other form of tangible, efficiently repeatable format is one of the most critical elements of becoming a successful leader of leaders.

Leaders of leaders must readily learn from those they lead. When the leader of leaders sets forth a platform, a principle, a rule, an approach to solving a class of problems, or a vision of what the future should be, the true leader of leaders must seek honest feedback regarding which parts of the platform works and which parts do not work. The leader of leaders must act decisively in changing, correcting, and improving those parts of the platform when notified that some of the platform is not helping achieve its goals. Because lawyers and personnel in legal organizations when acting as leaders of leaders must create platforms that guide their own behavior and inform their clients of their own approach to the law and serving clients, it is essential for lawyers who want to be leaders to establish individual platforms for themselves and their firms.

The first element of creating an individual platform is to be able to understand oneself well enough to understand one's strengths, weaknesses, key goals, and the values one will deploy in attempting to reach these goals. This requires reflection and the creation of a strong sense of identity on the part of the lawyer. This platform will serve not only as a guide to the lawyer, law firms, and all types of legal organizations, but also serve as a guide to the clients who seek the services of the lawyer and judges and tribunals where the lawyer practices.

Years ago, before lawyer advertising, a lawyer's or law firm's reputation and social contacts were the main sources of new business. We envision that when a lawyer or law firm explicitly constructs and communicates a platform to the legal community and potential clients, it will help the lawyer and firm develop a strong reputation for leadership effectiveness, which will give lawyers and firms a competitive advantage.

Of course, it is essential for a lawyer or firm that has created and communicated an individual platform to live and practice law in a manner consistent with the key elements of that platform. This platform will assist the lawyer in creating a long-term plan for the lawyer's legal career. Although a platform is designed to be a stable set of ideas and values, a platform is never static and cast in stone. It is an evolving, firmly rooted set of ideas, concepts, approaches, philosophy, ethics, and actions.

The idea of a personal or professional platform to guide one's professional life as a lawyer is neither new nor radical, but it is not often discussed in legal circles. Creating an individual platform upon which one's legal practice is based will profoundly affect one's identity. This platform can be used as an essential element by lawyers who seek to lead others and make a positive difference in this world.

In addition to creating individual platforms, creating an organizational platform is important in large organizations working in the legal profession including: law firms, government agencies, nonprofit organizations, and educational institutions. Moreover, there are many lawyers who are judges, mediators, arbitrators, fact finders, special investigative counsel, and "of counsel" who are asked, directly and indirectly, to shape the identity and personality of the organizations they serve. For these leaders in the legal profession the creation of an organizational platform would be an important element in using new leadership development strategies to improve the effectiveness of these organizations.

Today, lawyers, like many other leaders in the United States are primarily problem solvers. Very often, however, lawyers are called upon or volunteer to help organizations establish or change their strategic direction. Applied to the organizational context, a "platform" represents the core set of principles and values that a leader of leaders uses to set the tone, ethic, and direction of the organization as well as to figure out the best answers to systemic challenges and entire classes of problems an organization can face. Organizations that have explicit, well-accepted platforms are called "platform-driven organizations." It should be the goal of every legal organization to be a "platform driving organization."

The first characteristic of a platform-driven organization is that the platform is known, understood, respected, and dominant throughout the organization. It directs and guides decisions and actions at every moment and at every level. The second characteristic is that the platform is broad in scope and deep in meaning and impact. The third element is that the organizational platform is a living, breathing, streamlined set of values, principles, mores, and guidelines that leaders of the organization teach and model daily. The fourth key attribute of an organizational platform is that it inspires and demands consistent betterment of the entire organization.

Examples of sound organizational platforms are West Point and Washington and Lee University's honor codes; Nordstrom's customer service platform, "satisfy the customer;" IBM's platform in the 1980s "do what the customer needs;" and McKinsey's platform, "provide the client ten times greater value than the costs of the project." With the growing number of mergers between law firms, it is becoming increasingly difficult to identify the true platform of these merged organizations. Lawyers and all of the leaders of these newly merged law firms would serve their organizations well to work diligently to create a firm platform and encourage all lawyers and administrative staff to create their own personal platforms.

The creation, teaching, and enforcement of a true organizational platform represents a paradigm shift in the search to improve organizational effectiveness in the legal profession. This effort can prove to be very useful in regenerating trust within these organizations and improving the reputation of the legal profession itself. The steps described below show that it is challenging to create an organizational platform. However, because this platform will become the guiding set of principles used by leaders to lead their legal organizations, the effort to create such a platform cannot cut corners.

Below are twelve steps leaders of organizations undertake to become a platform-driven organization. These steps describe (1) how to create a robust platform; (2) how to implement the platform; and (3) how to refine and improve the platform.

1. Key leaders should develop a list of the core principles, obligations and objectives of the organization. The following are examples of a few items that might be included:

    a) Conduct all aspects of the law firm with the highest ethical standards.

    b) Perform thorough legal research identifying and analyzing all relevant law.

    c) Establish and maintain excellent service to all clients.

    d) Treat all employees with respect and dignity.

    e) Tell the truth in all circumstances regardless of the potential negative consequences.

    f) Strive to have the organization and each of its employees always seek excellence.

    g) Use technology to the organization's and clients' best advantage.

    h) Treat adversaries with respect and dignity, and demand that clients do the same.

    i) Work whenever possible in a team atmosphere and avoid silos.

2. After the major principles are identified and agreed upon, the next step in creating an organizational platform is to survey the key stakeholders, including all firm or agency employees, stockholders or equity partners, and major clients, to secure their input regarding the organizational platform.

3. The leaders then compile a more thorough list of ideas upon which an organizational platform should be based and develop a concise statement that embodies the core principles, obligations, and objectives of the organization. This document is the organization's draft platform.

4. The leaders then send out the organization's new platform to all key stakeholders for review and comment. They take all comments and revise and adopt this draft as the organizational platform. Then they distribute the platform broadly.

5. The organization, having adopted the organizational platform, then provides training to each employee and its clients on the meaning and role of the new platform and creates processes and procedures to make everyone accountable to the organization and to their fellow employees for implementing the platform meticulously.

6. The organization then publicizes the platform to clients and lets the world know the behaviors that the world can expect of the organization. Each member of the organization should sign a document stating full agreement with the platform. Violations of the platform should be deemed cause for dismissal or termination of any employee.

7. The organization then establishes a system to reward and regularly acknowledge examples of employee behavior consistent with the platform.

8. The organization also establishes a system to sanction any employee acting inconsistent with the platform and reward those who identify and report behavior that is not consistent with the platform.

9. The organization then continuously updates and disseminates examples of platform-consistent behaviors and platform-inconsistent behaviors.

10. The leaders of the organization must take quick, decisive, well-publicized, and strong action whenever platform-inconsistent behavior is observed in order to ensure that the person or group responsible for the platform-inconsistent behavior does not have the opportunity to act this way again in the organization.

11. The leaders of the organization should encourage all employees and stakeholders to provide feedback at every stage suggesting revisions in the platform.

12. The leaders should revise the platform regularly, and at least annually, to reflect feedback from stakeholders and republish, retain and reinvigorate the organization with the new, improved platform.

You will know when your organization does not have a platform just by asking the question of yourself and your organization's leaders, "What is our organization's platform?" Most often people who ask this question will not get a solid answer. Individuals in all organizations should ask, "What should our organization's platform be?" The answer to this question, once created and implemented throughout the organization, will become an important source of organizational betterment for all types of legal organizations.

Case Studies of the Distinction Between a Leader and a Leader of Leaders

After Howard T. Prince II returned from service in the U.S. Army in Vietnam he earned two of the most honored awards attainable by Army personnel. He became a Brigadier General in 1990 and received the Distinguished Service Award. When he began his leadership development work for the Army in 1978 as professor and head of the Department of Behavioral Sciences and Leadership at the U.S. Military Academy, West Point, he realized he had much work to do in the aftermath of the Vietnam War. While at West Point, Dr. Prince was the principal architect of both graduate and undergraduate leadership programs and was instrumental in reshaping leadership development training throughout the U.S. Army.

Dr. Prince knew that the Vietnam War had a profound, negative effect on Army leadership throughout the ranks all the way from the top down to the cadet level at West Point and enlisted persons. Integrity and telling the truth were severely compromised by many Army leaders during the Vietnam War. Understanding that the lack of integrity and the lack of a platform that insisted on telling the truth in every situation was very serious and potentially disabling to the Army in the long-run, presented Dr. Prince an enormous opportunity because he not only was a leader, he was a leader of leaders. By being a leader of leaders, he brought with him to his job at West Point a platform that included the highest ideals of service, integrity, and demand for accomplishment and accountability. Most importantly, his platform included honor, the honor of service, the honor of serving well, the honor of integrity and the honor of doing a difficult job meticulously when the environment the military faces is anything but meticulous.

Through living and teaching his platform of integrity and telling the truth regardless of the situation or consequences, he led the charge to reinstill the "ethic" of integrity into Army leadership training. From his days at the Army War College he learned the Uniform Code of Military Conduct. The magnitude of his duty could not have been more evident than when he faced the difficult task of interviewing 152 cadets at West Point who were expelled in a cheating scandal. He knew he had to reinvent a comprehensive leadership development program and a leadership culture based on the platform of integrity so that such a scandal could never occur again. Through Dr. Prince's leadership, his platform, and his ability to teach leadership and develop leaders, Dr. Prince's platform of integrity became again the Army's platform. It became the platform of every cadet that graduated from West Point while Dr. Prince was "on the watch" through 1990. His work shows the power of one man to see the challenges, identify the problems, and craft the proper solution. His work and his platform continued after he left West Point through his service as dean of the Jepson School of Leadership of the University of Richmond and as director of the Center for Ethical Leadership of the Lyndon B. Johnson School of Public Affairs of the University of Texas at Austin.

Not all individuals who are leaders of leaders are successful with all of their efforts. This second case study shows a leader of leaders who was fired by his board of directors. Soon after Dick Brown took over as Chief Executive Officer (CEO) of EDS he realized that EDS would not meet the analysts' earnings expectations. He immediately convened meetings to develop a plan to cut costs, a typical leader's response to short-term earnings problems. Then he sent an e-mail to everyone at EDS. Sending an e-mail to all 130,000 employees at EDS was no small task, because EDS used six different e-mail systems. Brown made sure that this problem was fixed so he could communicate whenever he wanted with every employee at EDS. His memo was simple and to the point. He told EDS employees of the earnings challenge and then asked each employee to identify how EDS could save $1,000, let him know what the employee recommended, and make a recommendation how EDS could accomplish this savings. It worked. Millions were saved virtually overnight. Brown created the platform that allowed all 130,000 people to work on a goal simultaneously. He created a system by which he could communicate with them and they could communicate with him and give him feedback. Then he immediately focused on improving revenues, which he understood required improving customer satisfaction.

The tale of J.C. Penney is different and shows the success of a leader of leaders. Allen Questrom became chairman and CEO of J.C. Penney. When he took over as CEO, J.C. Penney was languishing. The prevailing approach at J.C. Penney regarding management was decentralized, with the store managers making buying, advertising, and charitable contribution decisions. The result of this decentralization was that the "brand" of J.C. Penney was not uniformly presented to the world. Buying and other management decisions reflected more of the personal style of the store managers than the higher-ups at J.C. Penney. Questrom made a decision. He decided to centralize many activities and took power away from the store managers in the short run so that the central office could promote a consistent brand, create a philanthropic set of donations that furthered J.C. Penney's message, and make buying decisions more uniform. In just a few quarters, Questrom's new platform transformed J.C. Penney. In May 2002 its earnings report exceeded analysts' expectations by five cents per share. Questrom showed that he was a leader of leaders by creating a new platform, communicating that platform, getting his store managers to adopt the new platform, and producing great results in a short time.

The nonprofit world has its leaders of leaders. Mario Morino has done two things that place him in this category. First, he created "netpreneur.org," an organization that gave the Washington, D.C., area the "social infrastructure" to become a new-economy success story. He created the organization and set forth its rules, thus bringing together many leaders of the new economy to work together for the betterment of the area's economy and the many businesses located in the region. Morino created new rules, and a new paradigm for philanthropy as well, called "venture philanthropy." His platform, which is taking hold throughout the United States, is that foundations "invest" rather than make grants, that foundations must assist their grantees with managerial support, and that grantees should be entrepreneurial. They should carefully measure their efforts, plan strategically, meticulously track the funds they receive, and measure the impact of their efforts in improving communities and attacking social problems. Morino set out to improve the entire philanthropic industry, addressed a large class of issues the industry was facing, and created a framework to receive feedback from the industry to improve his social venture philanthropy platform.

Wendy Kopp is a leader of leaders in the nonprofit world. She created Teach for America, a program that recruits and trains, at some significant expense, students from the best colleges in the country to teach in the poorest public schools in the country, schools that are having difficulty in obtaining the teachers they need. The major expense of the program is the high cost of training these students to become teachers during the summer before their first teaching assignment and between their first and second years of teaching. As a leader of leaders, Kopp created a new platform or structure that redirected young college graduates who were intelligent, good students, and generally well-to-do, and gave them a platform that enabled them to teach and contribute to some of the lowest income students in the country.

In sum, it is the role of the organization's leaders and more importantly its leaders of leaders to create, disseminate, and enforce the platform for the organization. This important element has been missing from the organizational landscape and leadership development literature over the past several decades especially as it applies to the legal profession.

Law firms and other types of legal organizations are economic entities. They have a daily mission to serve the profession, their clients, and society as a whole. The creation of a platform is one form of road map that can influence behaviors, improve organizational performance, enhance the lives of those working for the organization, and reduce stress and conflict within organizations throughout the legal community.

CHAPTER THREE
LEADERSHIP BEHAVIORS AND MOTIVATION: PRACTICAL APPROACHES AND CHECKLISTS

In order to be a better leader, one needs to become familiar with examples of leadership behaviors that have proven successful over time. Within each category and specific behavioral item listed in this chapter, there is great room for individual variations and creativity. However, there is little room for the leader of a law firm, a leader of legal organizations, a leader of clients, or an advocate for a client to ignore the items listed below and still achieve passing marks in leadership. There are approximately sixty behaviors that researchers believe constitute good leadership practices.

Checklist 1: People Management

A successful leader is one who:

- ✓ Clearly communicates expectations
- ✓ Recognizes, acknowledges, and rewards achievement
- ✓ Inspires others and serves as a catalyst for others to perform in ways they would not undertake without the leader's support and direction
- ✓ Puts the right people in the right positions at the right time with the right resources and right job descriptions
- ✓ Secures alignment on what is the right direction for the organization
- ✓ Persuades and encourages people in the organization to achieve the desired results for the organization
- ✓ Makes sure not to burn out people in the organization, looking out for their well being as well as the well-being of the organization

- ✓ Identifies weak signals that suggest impending conflict within the organization and attacks the sources of conflict effectively

- ✓ Holds people accountable

- ✓ Encourages the human capital development of every person in the organization through training, mentoring, and education, and allocates sufficient resources to this endeavor

- ✓ Correctly evaluates the actual performance and the potential of each person in the organization

- ✓ Encourages people in the organization to stand up for and express their beliefs

- ✓ Creates a non-fear-based environment in which all persons in the organization can speak the truth as they see it without concern for retaliation

- ✓ Is able to empathize with those he or she leads

Checklist 2: Strategic Management

A successful leader is one who:

- ✓ Is flexible when necessary to adapt to changing circumstances

- ✓ Sets, with input from others including all stakeholders, the long-term direction for the organization

- ✓ Understands the organization's competitive environment, social trends, competitors, customers, and all stakeholders

- ✓ Correctly analyzes the potential risks of all decisions

- ✓ Correctly analyzes the potential returns of all decisions

- ✓ Has the ability to focus on specific problems without losing his or her ability to see at the outer edges, gathering worthwhile information that others miss or fail to see as significant or relevant

- ✓ Understands the strengths and weaknesses of the organization and how to exploit the strengths and address the weaknesses successfully
- ✓ Develops and implements strategies to improve the strengths and to combat the weaknesses of the organization
- ✓ Identifies appropriate partners, strategic alliances, and outside resources to tap in order to help further the organization's goals
- ✓ Articulates the values of the organization and develops strategies consistent with these core values
- ✓ Demonstrates a strong commitment to diversity and positive change
- ✓ Demonstrates a strong commitment to creating and sustaining a learning organization (learning is the foundation for all sustainable change)

Checklist 3: Personal Characteristics

A successful leader is one who:

- ✓ Lives with honesty and integrity
- ✓ Selects people for his or her team who are honest and have high integrity
- ✓ Has the will, passion, and desire to succeed
- ✓ Possesses a willingness to shoulder the responsibility for success (without being a "thunder taker") and failure (without casting blame)
- ✓ Is innovative and open to new ideas
- ✓ Is not willing to accept the ways things are because they can always be improved; is never satisfied completely with the status quo
- ✓ Is smart, intelligent, emotionally strong

- ✓ Is confident without being arrogant
- ✓ Is an able negotiator
- ✓ Is willing to be patient
- ✓ Is decisive when necessary
- ✓ Is able to think analytically
- ✓ Learns quickly
- ✓ Is respectful to all
- ✓ Is perceptive and sensitive to the needs of others
- ✓ Demonstrates diligence, discipline, and strong perseverance capabilities
- ✓ Is comfortable with ambiguity
- ✓ Is willing to be original
- ✓ Takes informed and intelligent risks

Checklist 4: Process Management

A successful leader is one who:

- ✓ Manages change
- ✓ Promotes innovation
- ✓ Secures resources
- ✓ Allocates resources wisely
- ✓ Solves problems well
- ✓ Anticipates crises
- ✓ Handle crises well when they explode
- ✓ Creates and manages budgets well
- ✓ Creates and manages timelines and work plans

- ✓ Possesses and manifests great project management skills
- ✓ Translates long-term visions into step-by-step plans
- ✓ Measures results and reports them accurately
- ✓ Recognizes quickly when a process or activity is not working
- ✓ Redesigns processes as often as necessary to be successful

These leadership behaviors and categories apply to lawyers and people in the legal profession just as they apply to leaders in every profession and organization. One might want to rate oneself and others on a scale of 1 to 10 on each of these leadership abilities. Individuals in the legal profession might also want to use "360 degree feedback," asking those with whom they work, including peers, superiors, and subordinates, to rate them on each of these skills and abilities.

Knowing the full extent of this checklist may remind the lawyer and those in the legal profession of the importance of certain leadership behaviors that they may not have considered important in the past. Each skill or ability can be learned and can be improved. Self-awareness of one's strengths and weaknesses is a first step toward improvement and improving leadership. This list of leadership behaviors can be used by all types of legal organizations as criteria to evaluate their employees and their leaders. Workshops and seminars can be taken to improve each of these skills and we recommend that such education and training programs be approved for CLE credit. Now we turn to an area of leadership that has not received much attention in the legal profession: motivation.

Motivation Explained and Demonstrated

Literature from 1974 provides some useful guidance on motivating oneself and others. House and Mitchell[2] in their article "Path-Goal Theory of Leadership" state that leadership generates motivation when the leaders show that he or she has the power and influence to improve situations and undertakes the following behaviors:

1. is willing and able to increase the kinds of payoffs that subordinates want,

2. shows its willingness to create rapport with subordinates,

3. works to make the subordinate's jobs easier and more likely to be successful,

4. makes sacrifices on behalf of subordinates,

5. gives acknowledgement appropriately, and

6. creates goals and objectives that are intrinsically appealing to subordinates.

Research on motivation shows that the following twenty-two factors are all essential to creating environmental conditions supportive of leaders motivating those they lead.

1. Subordinates understand the goals of the group and its leaders.

2. Subordinates know what is expected of them.

3. Leaders maintain a friendly yet disciplined relationship with subordinates.

4. Leaders consult with subordinates.

5. Leaders coach and mentor subordinates.

6. Leaders listen actively to subordinates.

---

[2] R.J. House and T.R. Mitchell, "Path-Goal Theory of Leadership," *Journal of Contemporary Business* 3 (1974): 81-97.

LEADERSHIP BEHAVIORS AND MOTIVATION

7. Leaders keep subordinates accurately informed.

8. Leaders exhibit the same ethics they demand of subordinates and are trusted by subordinates.

9. Leaders endeavor to understand the situation the subordinates face.

10. Leaders set realistic individual and collective goals for subordinates and challenge subordinates in a way that engenders strong, positive responses.

11. Leaders take into account the feelings and emotions of subordinates and try to accommodate their personal needs.

12. Leaders give encouragement to subordinates.

13. Leaders help subordinates become better problem solvers.

14. Leaders tell the truth to subordinates and demand the same from them.

15. Leaders deliver punishment effectively when warranted.

16. Leaders are perceived by subordinates as being fair.

17. Leaders create a vision for subordinates that both is realistic, comprehensible, and challenges their imagination.

18. Leaders use humor appropriately.

19. Leaders express appropriate confidence in subordinates.

20. Leaders know the capabilities of their subordinates, demand that they perform at their highest levels, and let subordinates know that the leader is monitoring their activities against that standard.

21. Leaders undertake substantial effort to help subordinates grow into leaders.

22. Leaders resign when they fail or when their subordinates are not motivated to success by the leader's actions, thus allowing another leader to take the reins.

Certainly, being able to motivate oneself and others requires additional important attributes, including the following:

- Recognizing and avoiding burnout in oneself and others
- Improving the ability of participants to delegate and achieve results through the work and cooperation of others
- Articulating and understanding group dynamics, followership, and factors in communications styles, strategies, and content that affect the response of others
- Recognizing the power of building long-lasting professional relationships
- Implementing strategies to create and elicit rapport
- Appreciating the value of one's reputation and its relationship to motivation
- Calling forth the leadership potential in others and in oneself
- Knowing the role of fair and equitable treatment of others in achieving and maintaining high motivation.

Motivation is a critical component of leadership. In the legal community, lawyers and leaders of legal organizations are called upon every day to motivate associates, motivate staff, motivate court clerks and personnel to perform their duties well, motivate their clients to help gather facts and witnesses, and motivate themselves to serve as models in the community. Although people may believe that teaching motivation skills is difficult, this chapter has outlined many of the basic elements that go into successful efforts to motivate others. Lawyers and people working in the legal profession with their heavy work schedules, demanding clients and judges, challenging cases, and large areas of responsibility would be well served to understand some of the key theories and basic underpinnings of motivation and become better motivators. Each person in the legal profession will need to find an approach to motivation that works in a repeatable fashion over time. Motivation is a key element in avoiding burnout and in producing great results in teams and workplaces. Lawyers are faced with one type of a motivation-oriented problem that is rarely faced by any other professional. Because lawyers work in an adversary system, lawyers must often motivate their adversaries, motivate third parties such as juries and judges, and motivate government agencies and other tribunals to treat their clients fairly. Thus, the arenas where lawyers earn their living have special motivation-oriented challenges far beyond the challenges faced by most workers and most professions in our economy.

CHAPTER FOUR
THE ETHICS OF LEADERSHIP

Lawyers and the entire legal profession have a special relationship with ethics. Because lawyers, judges, arbitrators, mediators, and many others in the legal profession occupy positions of great power and influence, ethics has been a mainstay of legal education, codes of professional responsibility, and a lawyer's or law firm's reputation for centuries. This chapter pays special tribute to the current and evolving role that ethics plays in the legal profession. Because there is no general theory of ethical leadership in the leadership literature, this chapter focuses on how ethics has evolved in the legal profession and how it can evolve in the future to support the desires of lawyers and members of the legal profession to be better leaders.

The ethical rules for lawyers are detailed and teaching ethics to lawyers relies heavily on examples where lawyers were not ethical. Efforts to provide general ethical rules have been codified in legal texts for many decades. Yet, many lawyers are looking for new ethical guidelines that can supplement the ethics courses they are required to take each and every year.

Almost all states require some education in ethics annually. The fifth edition of the *Annotated Model Rules of Professional Conduct* runs 721 pages.[3] The ABA has a standing committee on ethics and professional responsibility, and the first rule of the Model Rules after "Competence" is the "Allocation of Authority Between Client and Lawyer." Rule 1.2(a) is clear: "… a lawyer shall abide by a client's decisions concerning the objectives of the representation."[4] In two other instances, this rule uses the terms "shall abide by a client's decision." However, there is a huge caveat in this general rule, because the rule begins, "Subject to paragraphs (c) and (d) … ." Paragraph (c) goes to the issue of

---
3 American Bar Association, *Annotated Model Rules of Professional Conduct*, 5th ed. (Center for Professional Responsibility, American Bar Association, 2002).
4 Ibid., 27.

limiting representation if that limitation is "reasonable." Paragraph (d) states, "A lawyer shall not counsel a client to engage, or to assist a client, in conduct that the lawyer knows to be criminal or fraudulent ...".[5]

This rule sets the minimum standard of behavior or "platform" by which a lawyer must always abide without exception. The commentary is clear; lawyers must avoid "suggesting how the wrongdoing may be concealed."[6] Lawyers cannot even provide "passive assistance, such as withholding information from a court or government tribunal."[7] A lawyer may never advise a client to commit a criminal or fraudulent act.[8] No lawyers or any person in the legal profession is ever allowed to help a client pursue an unlawful objective or counsel unlawful behavior by lying or deceit.

Rule 2.1 of the Model Rules states, "... a lawyer shall exercise independent professional judgment and render candid advice. In rendering advice, a lawyer may refer not only to the laws but to other considerations such as moral, economic, social and political factors, that may be relevant to the client's situation."[9] An important first question then is, what is meant by the term "exercise independent professional judgment"? Clearly this term means the lawyer must abide by the ethical rules of our profession notwithstanding the client's objectives. Thus lawyers and the legal professionals are never to serve merely as vehicles for achieving all of the client's wishes regardless of whether they are criminal or fraudulent. The commentary to the ethical rules of the legal profession is clear: "It is proper for a lawyer to refer to relevant moral and ethical considerations in giving advice."[10]

It is useful to ask where does the lawyer obtain information on these "moral and ethical considerations"? Not from law school. Not from continuing legal education.[11] A lawyer certainly gets this

---

5 Ibid., 27.
6 Ibid., 39.
7 Ibid.
8 Ibid.
9 Ibid., 289.
10 Ibid.
11 This author has found no course offered in law school called "Moral and Ethical Considerations" nor has he found such a course in his review of CLE programs. The author acknowledges that courses are offered on the biblical and Judaic sources of many of our laws in force today, but we find no primers in law school on morals. We are not suggesting that law schools should teach such courses. We are only showing the need that each person in the legal profession has to develop individual platforms and organizational platforms based on morals and ethical considerations before lawyers can competently meet the test and requirements of Rule 2.1 and serve as leaders of leaders.

THE ETHICS OF LEADERSHIP

information on moral and ethical considerations from his or her upbringing, education, and daily life. However, unless and until such moral and ethical considerations are put into a lawyer's or law firm's platform, a client can never be certain that the advice based on moral and ethical considerations will be consistent over time from an individual lawyer, a law firm, or across law firms.

The Model Rules even provide leadership guidance in the law firm setting. Rule 5.2 states, in effect, that a subordinate lawyer is not in violation of the rules of professional conduct if he or she does what a supervising lawyer tells him or her to do after the supervising lawyer has attempted to make a "reasonable resolution of an arguable question of professional duty."[12] This rule makes the more senior attorney totally accountable in this situation and limits the responsibility of the junior lawyer unless the junior lawyer knew what he or she was doing violated the rules of professional conduct.

These rules related to supervision are needed to protect subordinate lawyers for several reasons. First, the rules are challenging for many lawyers. Second, the legal profession is strongly supportive of individual responsibility, and this set of rules clearly places individual responsibility for the acts of junior lawyers on the shoulders of the senior lawyers who gave them orders. Third, these rules implicitly acknowledge the reality that senior lawyers exercise "power over" (more than they exercise "power with") subordinate lawyers. The leadership style of most law firms and most organizations where lawyers work is hierarchical. Some law firms, government agencies, corporate legal departments, and other entities where lawyers work are beginning to use consultative leadership, participative leadership and other forms of shared leadership. However, regardless of the legal setting, in the United States the "command" and "control" style of leadership is still predominant in these settings and Rule 5.2 reflects that fact.

This chapter examines the emerging "ethics" of command and control forms of leadership. Rule 1.2 (abiding by the client's objectives) is designed to prevent lawyers from exercising command and control leadership over their clients. Rule 1.2(d) (no counsel for criminal conduct) is designed, as is Rule 2.1 (independent judgment), from keeping the client from exercising command and

---
12 Model Rules, 449.

control leadership over the lawyer. The essence of Rule 1.2 is that the lawyer can do nothing of a substantial nature affecting the rights of the client without the client's informed consent. This is the ultimate statement of participatory leadership and consultative leadership. Similarly, doctors are not able to make any medical decisions that substantially affect the well-being of a patient without informed consent expressly given by the patient (emergencies excepted). Thus, the bedrock, but often forgotten, leadership principle of both the medical and legal professions is the doctrine of participatory leadership. Stated simply, both professions hold that it is unethical to make a decision that affects a client's or patient's life without giving that client or patient a meaningful chance to participate in the decision-making process (again, emergencies excepted). This is the evolving standard in leadership development today. Certainly there are times, more in the medical profession than in the legal profession, when due to an emergency, the lawyer or doctor must make and execute a key life or death decision without the client's informed consent. Yet, the key principle of consultative or participatory leadership still holds.

The predominant challenge to the field of leadership ethics is that ethics is basically "a standard by which we measure behavior." There are billions of behaviors every second in the world, and it is impossible to create a set of ethical principles to apply to each behavior. The result is either "ethical relativism" or "ethical absolutism." Neither ethical relativism, with porous boundaries, nor ethical absolutism with rigid walls, is satisfactory. Thus, there is no general theory of ethical leadership today.

There is a new approach to ethics that should be of particular interest to lawyers in leadership positions. It is grounded in Rules 1.2 and 2.1 of the Model Rules. It is also grounded in the fact that lawyers are trained in legal analysis, advocacy, the technical legal requirements of certain transactions, in reading and understanding the history, the present, and the reasonable future projections of the law, all in order to advise clients on how to behave and make decisions that support the notion of a lawful and orderly society. Lawyers are trained to interpret documents and defend and ascertain the rights of individuals, including those who have violated the laws of society. This legal training gives lawyers special insights and special blind spots. For lawyers, the commentary to the Model Rules states, "Advice couched in narrow legal terms may be of little value to the client, especially where practical considerations, such as cost or effects on other people, are predominant. Purely technical advice, therefore, can sometimes be inadequate."[13] This passage should be read as a warning to lawyers that something very important might be missing from legal training and even legal experience. The premise of this book is that one of the things missing from the legal profession today is a solid foundation in leadership theory and practice and the ethics of leadership.

The new ethics of leadership that is emerging, rather than focusing on evaluating behavior, focuses on evaluting how decisions are made. In the next fifty years, lawyers' fact-finding roles will be greatly reduced by DNA testing, surveillance cameras, electronic mail, and computer documentation of activities leading up to actions and transactions. Although the presentation of such evidence is still quite cumbersome given the slowly changing rules of evidence, during the next ten to twenty years, surveillance cameras, black boxes in automobiles, photo cameras at intersections where accidents often occur, people with home video cameras and electronic surveillance of conversations will all be enhanced. When there is a dispute as to who did what to whom, some significant electronic evidence will often be available to the tribunal in the future. Then, rather than who did what, the issue will be, how do we deal with the fact that X person did Y thing which runs afoul of the law?

The new ethics of leadership then will focus on the ethics of decision making, well rooted in law and medicine. The new rule of ethical leadership will be "In most circumstances the better approach, the more ethical approach, in making a decision that affects other people's lives is to give them an opportunity to participate in the decision-making process." Certainly many leaders have been suggesting this for years. Yet, the command and control form of leadership is the opposite of this new type of ethical leadership that demands inclusion of all people who will be affected in the decision-making process. Clearly, this new ethical approach to leadership and decision-making will represent a new way of doing business for many lawyers, and the legal profession itself.

---

13   Model Rules, 289.

How does this new ethical approach affect the practice of law when lawyers are called upon to be leaders? This idea of participatory decision making will require more openness (inclusion) with clients and even with opposing counsel and adversaries. This new ethical approach to leadership requires consultation and negotiation, rather than merely leveraging power to accomplish a client's ends.

There are still many law firms with greater than ten lawyers where one or two senior partners make all compensation decisions, all hiring and firing decisions, and most of the strategic decisions in client matters. Perhaps this was a good strategy a century ago. However, with the improvement in the education of lawyers and clients, the broadening of young lawyers' desire to be meaningful participants in law firm and legal organization's governance, their strong ability to provide useful intelligence to aid decision makers, and their improved leadership skills, all contribute to the growing convergence between the new leadership ethics espoused by this book and the new schools of management philosophy developing across the United States. This new leadership ethic calls for greater inclusion of lawyers at all levels of the firm or legal organization in making key decisions. This new leadership ethic calls for greater client involvement in the decisions that ultimately affect the strategy and approach used in pursuit of the client's goals. This new leadership ethic calls into question the basic validity of command and control leadership which is still the predominant style of leadership practiced throughout the legal profession.

There are times when it is necessary for command and control leadership to be used, especially when emergencies occur. However, the management rationale, the business rationale, and the legal industry's rationale, often unspoken, about why the first name on the door makes all key decisions is now contradicted by modern leadership theory and practice. For many who have exercised command and control leadership, including micromanagement, giving up the reins will not be easy. People who have never been part of a serious decision-making process will have a tough learning curve. Know-it-all leaders will have to realize that others in the firm or organization can improve the quality of their decision making through their active participation. The ethics of leadership now requires leaders to improve the qualities and capabilities of the "followership." Often, clients are followers. Junior lawyers, administrators, marketing directors, paralegals, secretaries, and vendors are all followers. In order for these people to know who and what to follow, they need the guidance of an organizational platform and the opportunity to participate meaningfully in all key decisions that affect the law firm.

The teaching of leadership in organizations is also undergoing a transformation that will have a direct impact on law firms. In 2004, in a breakthrough training agreement, Reed Smith signed a large contract with the Wharton School at the University of Pennsylvania to teach members of the law firm leadership principles and skills. Although the provisions of the contract are confidential, the fact that the Wharton School was hired to teach Reed Smith's lawyers and key staff leadership development was publicly disclosed. To our knowledge, it was the first contract of its kind in which a law firm paid substantial sums to a noted leadership development organization to teach leadership skills to large numbers of lawyers and other staff in the firm. Although the results of the program are still unknown, the firm and those in the leadership development industry believe that Reed Smith will reap substantial competitive advantages from this investment in its lawyers and staff. Other law firms are now following in Reed Smith's footsteps with contracts with Harvard to teach the law firm members leadership.

Thus, we are entering into a new era of leadership and ethics in the law firm setting and in the legal profession. New standards are evolving not only as to what is ethical behavior, but what is ethical decision making. The command and control environment of the past two hundred years in the legal profession is coming under increasing pressure and scrutiny. New forms of ethical decision-making structures will appear as law firms, corporate counsel offices, and other legal organizations expand the circle of those in the organization allowed to participate in a meaningful way in making key decisions in client matters, law firm, and organizational management matters. Similarly, in the corporations and nonprofit organizations where lawyers wield power, these changes are now or soon will be taking place. Lawyers will be called upon more than ever before to be leaders and to involve followers in the decision-making process, rather than simply calling out orders to follow and expecting everyone in the organization to accept every decision of those at the top and carry out their every command. When lawyers want to excel as leaders, they will be well served to master this new participatory leadership model. Because the quality of a lawyer's work is often the direct result of the decisions the lawyer makes or helps shape, lawyers now have an ethical duty to employ decision-making structures that have been proven to improve decisions. That decision-making approach is called participatory or consultative decision making.

CHAPTER FIVE
TEACHING LEADERSHIP IN THE LEGAL PROFESSION THE NEW MODEL

Stating that lawyers should learn more about leadership development and should improve their leadership skills in order to improve their success and satisfaction as lawyers and managers is easy. It is much more difficult to prescribe exactly how to accomplish these goals. This chapter asks and begins to answer the question, "How can legal organizations begin to learn and teach leadership skills and principles in a cost-effective manner and thus improve the leadership skills and aptitude of those at all levels of the profession?"

Certainly the leadership development profession stands ready to serve the legal community. Currently it is a $4-billion-per-year industry and could provide its standard in-person, online, team-oriented, or individual-coaching leadership curriculum to law firms. In fact, one company, IBM, has developed so many leadership courses for middle managers in the nonlegal sectors that it charges approximately $1 million for the purchase of the "asset," which comprises the courses, the electronic learning platform, and the learning management system that helps determine who needs what courses through rigorous assessment. This system also tracks what leadership courses each person takes and how they affect his or her workplace performance. All customization, and much is required to fine tune the leadership courses to the culture of the workplace and its prevalent leadership styles, raises the cost of this leadership development program to well over $1 million.

This chapter explains how leadership is often taught in corporations and provides a new paradigm that will be much more cost-effective and much more productive in law firms, for in-house counsel, agency, or court settings. There will always be the need for executive coaching designed to help an individual become a better leader and become more conscious of his or her own leadership strengths and weaknesses. There will always be hundreds of leadership assessment tools that ask the respondent how he or she would react in certain situations and what he or she thinks about certain issues. These tools can be highly instructive for those who are not aware of many of the behavioral dimensions and leadership strategies that they use currently or are or not aware of more successful approaches.

There is also be great value for people in the legal profession to study the various leadership approaches and behavioral styles of team-oriented leadership. These can show how different people can work successfully with each other in a team setting in ways that might not be possible unless each person is trained to understand the personalities and behavioral and leadership preferences that each person on the team possesses. Similarly, there will be value in studies of leadership preferences and styles of everyone in an organization and an assessment of the culture of the organization that will help identify those people who operate in ways that are currently outside the mainstream of the organization's culture.

This chapter takes a new approach to the teaching of leadership, one different from that is typically used in the leadership consulting profession. Although we have defined leadership previously, there is one important added dimension to teaching leadership to members of an organization. One goal of teaching leadership is to teach the students of the leadership course how to instruct others in the organization regarding leadership. It can be said that a key element of leadership is "repeatability." A leader has a direct impact on a follower or group of followers when these followers "repeat" the behavior of the leader. This does not mean that followers become robots. Quite the contrary. In this instance, followers act in the way that they perceive the leader would want them to act in that situation. Having a platform is critical here because platforms are created not by one person, but by the contributions of all stakeholders. The platform is known, is discussed, and becomes part of the culture so it can affect the members of the organization as they serve their clients, their organization, and their profession.

TEACHING LEADERSHIP IN THE LEGAL PROFESSION—THE NEW MODEL

Leadership training today in organizations usually follows a similar process. Only a few at the top of the organization receive this training. Once they receive this training, they are supposed to be better leaders. However, in most cases, they are not expected to use this leadership training to train others in the organization. Therefore, in order for all employees to receive leadership training, the training company will recommend that it receive a contract that will allow it to provide leadership training to each and every lawyer and staff member in small group settings. This approach is highly inefficient.

It would be much more efficient to create leadership development courses that law firms, companies, nonprofit organizations, and educational institutions can pay for once with only a portion of their employees taking the course. Then the employees who take the leadership development course could teach other lawyers and employees in the firm the material and lessons they have learned. This type of leadership development training course and improved leadership behaviors learned by the "early adopters" in the firm could replicate themselves within the organization through organic growth.

This teaching model for leadership is uniquely suited for a professional services firm like a law firm and other legal organizations in the profession. It would be a much more evolutionary process than the leadership development profession currently uses, where outsiders teach either only those few at the top or teach each and every person in the firm in small groups. When those in the firm who learn leadership development become teachers in the firm as individual mentors and as classroom instructors, the teachings are handed down from generation to generation in the firm and from lawyer to lawyer and employee to employee. Such a process would not only be more efficient than the current leadership development teaching model, this type of process would serve as a "glue" bonding teacher to learner (employee to employee) throughout the organization. This leadership development teaching process would reduce turnover; reduce associate dissatisfaction; promote mentoring, improved collegiality, and reduced competition among lawyers in the same firm. It would help break down silos that can occur across practice groups and across offices in different cities. This learning model would also be much more cost-effective than traditional leadership development training.

Certainly not every lawyer or staff member in a firm who takes one or more courses in leadership development will become an effective teacher of leadership skills. Some people who take leadership development courses may not be good students and may not change their behavior significantly after taking these courses. However, on the whole, this instructional model in which students become teachers of leadership development is actually well suited to the highly educated environment of law firms and legal organizations. The potential value that the adoption of this model of leadership development education could provide to lawyers and employees makes this model both intuitively appealing and efficient. Lawyers and legal staffs face great time demands. By creating leadership development courses using leadership development instructors within the firm, and with leadership development practitioners who understand the time demands on lawyers, firms will be able to make the proper scheduling decisions so that the lawyers and employees of the firm or legal organization can properly juggle client demands, law firm demands, organizational demands, and the time it takes for proper leadership development training and teaching.

There are many specific steps that a law firm can adopt in the development and execution of a leadership course for its lawyers and all staff. In fact, some law firms or legal organizations may find it useful to create a strategic alliance or a joint venture with other law firms or legal organizations and take and develop leadership courses together or in groups. Bar associations may assist small firms and sole practitioners in joining together under a bar association banner to participate not only in the first round of leadership development instruction led by a recognized leadership instructor, but also the second and third rounds of instruction that are at least, in part, taught by the lawyers and legal staffs that participated in the first round of instruction. Even sole practitioners could well benefit from going through the process of creating a leadership platform and securing leadership development training for themselves because they are often called upon to lead client organizations, individual clients, and adversaries in litigation, arbitration, and mediation settings.

Leadership development courses for law firms and other legal organizations should include the following objectives:

1. ***Define*** the terms and vocabulary of leadership

2. ***Comprehend*** the meaning of leadership from many theoretical and practical perspectives

3. ***Apply*** the knowledge base that has been developed in the field of leadership so that in real situations the students will be able to develop and implement the most appropriate leadership behavior for themselves and for those they lead

4. ***Analyze*** situations to know which type of leadership behavior will be most effective for the situation

5. ***Synthesize*** all of the knowledge in the course on leadership so that those enrolled will develop confidence in their ability to lead and teach others to lead successfully

6. ***Evaluate*** leadership acts so that those enrolled will know very quickly whether the leaders (either themselves or another leader) are being successful and how to improve their leadership behaviors

7. ***Use*** experiential examples and exercises so students can observe the other participants take on leadership challenges and be able to give them honest feedback on how they performed when faced with leadership challenges

Leadership development courses for people in the legal profession should be both intellectual and vocational. Those enrolled in the course should be expected to begin demonstrating improved leadership behaviors immediately upon taking the course in their personal and professional lives.

Leadership development courses for the legal community should be designed to stimulate participants to become "learners" in the field of leadership, as well as teachers of leadership to others in the firm or legal organization. Leadership development courses for the legal community should encourage those enrolled to continue independent leadership study, exercises, group discussions, rigorous self-assessment, and assessment of others' leadership behaviors.

These leadership development courses should be designed to promote the willingness, eagerness, and interest of the participants in taking on greater and greater leadership responsibilities than they would have been willing to do previously. Ultimately, these leadership development courses should enable participants to become teachers of leadership in a short period of time.

Many people working in law firms and legal organizations have had nearly twenty years of formal education. Traditional lecture formats will not be sufficient to teach leadership development to the legal profession. Courses on leadership development, as well as motivation, must be innovative and use advanced pedagogical techniques such as the following:

1. Role playing and simulations of the leadership styles and brands outlined in this book and opportunities for honest feedback, second tries, and discussion of the improvements and shortcomings of the participants (in private or in groups)

2. Visual diagrams of leadership theories, leadership brands, and leadership checklists in addition to text-based learning tools

3. Group and individual exercises that encourage and reward participants to increase their willingness to participate in leadership activities

4. Detailed examples showing how poor leadership behaviors can create unfortunate results for clients, law firms, legal organizations, the public at large, and the individual lawyers and legal staffs involved

5. Written assignments identifying the leadership behaviors of the best leaders with whom they have worked in their past; homework assignments; and writing memos explaining the particular leadership styles or theories of leadership that most appeal to the participant

6. An assessment of how the individual participant's leadership style and behaviors fits in or conflicts with the organizational platform

7. A rigorous feedback system by which others in the organization who work with the participant regularly assess and comment upon improvements or the lack of improvement in leadership behaviors and aptitude

8. Asking participants to create a leadership workbook or diary to write down changes in their leadership behaviors

9. Asking participants to develop their own list of leadership "best practices" and sharing them on a regular basis with colleagues

10. A scheduling system for leadership development courses that employs rigor and discipline and at the same time recognizes the need for lawyers and legal staff to deal effectively with client and organizational demands and emergencies

11. Creation of leadership groups who will work together on projects with each person taking turns at being the leader; each group would generate a written report, "Leadership in Action: Lessons Learned and Results Achieved," to share with other participants

12. Working with those participants who want to serve as future teachers of a leadership development course to develop their own "teacher's guide" for later use

These teaching methods and suggested course of study in the field of leadership development are innovative. They are rigorous and demanding. They are based on the premise that knowledge and the appreciation of the benefits of additional knowledge, aptitude, and skill in the area of leadership are fundamental prerequisites to action learning. Leadership development courses for those in the legal profession must be designed so those enrolled generate and maintain strong will to become better leaders and demand that others around them become better leaders as well.

For those in the legal profession who want to enroll in or create courses on motivation, as well as leadership, there are several guidelines to share. Given the very high burnout rate among lawyers, and the long work hours for both lawyers and legal staffs, a course in motivation theory and practice would be quite important.

One might ask whether this teaching of leadership development and motivation could create disharmony in legal workplaces. Put more bluntly, could it foster an employee revolution? For the reasons below, the author believes that such courses are much more likely to create useful employee evolution and betterment rather than employee revolution.

Leadership has been previously defined in this book as *the creation and fulfillment of worthwhile opportunities by honorable means.* In other words, leadership is all about making a contribution to the business, the nonprofit organization, the educational organization, the law firm, the organizations in the legal profession, and the legal profession, clients, and society as a whole. This definition of leadership applies to one's family, community, and in all institutions where one participates as well. Unfortunately, somewhere in the historical evolution of leadership theory and practice, people got off track and leadership became reserved for the few, the elite. However, whether we call it democracy, transparency, diversity, liberalism, inclusion, participatory leadership, servant leadership, quality circles, or any other name, the clear evolutionary process unfolding before us is a shift away from anointing only a small cadre to assume all leadership roles and making all key decisions to focusing on how to get more people (including employees, lawyers, and staff) involved in leadership.

TEACHING LEADERSHIP IN THE LEGAL PROFESSION—THE NEW MODEL

These leadership development courses and this book will provide an opportunity to train individuals in law firms and other organizations in the legal profession to assume more responsibility for leading, teaching leadership behaviors, mentoring, and helping establish "platforms" for the organizations. These courses could also play an important role in improving services to the clients, improving financial results, and improving other measures of success for the organization.

Young professionals, be they staff or lawyers in legal organizations, want distributed leadership. They have been leaders in their student organizations, in volunteer efforts, in their churches and synagogues, in their families, and in their academic classes. They know, in some small way, how to lead, and even though they may not know how to lead clients in complex matters, how to lead law firms in the new legal business environment, or how to lead judges or administrative tribunals through an arduous trial. They know they want to be part of the leadership team and they want to participate in a meaningful way in the decisions that affect their lives both professionally and personally. They know they are capable of filling a position someday where they can be a leader of leaders, and they will not wait ten years in any organization to step up to the plate to lead in important situations. They view law school and the training they received for the positions they now hold in legal organizations as their apprenticeship time, and they want to be given substantial responsibility, significant opportunities to be trained to be leaders, and a real chance to be a leader on projects that require the coordinated work of many people. To withhold leadership training and not allow these people to assume leadership positions in legal organizations are sure ways to waste important talent.

Similarly, the legal clients of today want highly motivated, independent professionals who are customer or client oriented, punctual, responsive, and who treat them with dignity and respect. They want legal professionals who have a strong platform that embodies a clear sense of moral and ethical considerations and learning, and they want their counsel and legal staffs to have integrity, be credible, and be totally proficient in their trade. Leadership training and motivation training is designed to enhance each of these areas of human development. People are not born leaders. The idea of the "self-made person" is not only a myth, it is as ludicrous as the story about Abraham Lincoln, about whom it was once said, "He was born in a log cabin that he built himself."

Not only has this chapter described how to teach leadership development in the context of the legal profession, it also has opened the door to the answer to Judge Barr's question regarding whether improving the leadership skills of lawyers would in fact make these lawyers better lawyers. Although the jury is still out on this central question, the final section of this book tackles that question, both in theory and through the use of reasoning and logic. There is a new leadership calculus emerging in the world. That calculus simply stated is *"All other things being equal, the more people who participate in the leadership of an organization and make worthwhile contributions to that organization, the greater the output of the organization will be, the more efficient the organization will be, and the better the organization will perform."*

This increased quantity of leadership (more people participating in the leadership of legal organizations) creates an increase in the quality of leadership. Recognition of this emerging truth in the legal profession will spur the training and improvement of leaders and leadership. We will see leadership development programs and opportunities in law firms and in organizations in the legal profession grow from the few to the many over the next decade. Information technology, which will make it more efficient for more people to be involved in the decision-making process, will certainly fuel this new emphasis on fostering leadership behaviors.

Teaching Leadership for Lawyers: The Potential Future Role of Bar Associations and Continuing Legal Education Providers

For these reasons, there is also a strong business case that can be made for bar associations and other private continuing legal education providers to begin providing leadership development courses for lawyers right away. Although the leadership development literature and educational sectors have been booming over the past ten years and entering into new discipline after new discipline (e.g., engineering, psychology, public policy, etc.), the legal sector of our economy has not invested to date in training its professionals in leadership development to any great extent.

In approximately forty states, state bar associations require lawyers to take between ten and fifteen hours of continuing legal education annually (or thirty or so hours over three years). Most of these courses involve particular technical aspects of the law from "How to Take Depositions" to updates on the changes in the law in subject matter areas where many lawyers specialize and where general practitioners need these courses to stay up-to-date. At the conference of the Association of Continuing Legal Education Administrators in Denver, Colorado, in August 2004 a distinguished panel concluded that lawyers both in large law firms and in small and solo practices selected particular continuing legal education courses for five basic reasons:

1. The content/information of the course was considered "timely" and of "critical importance" to the lawyer who needed information on this topic at or near the time the course was offered.

2. The course sponsor and/or course leader was considered by the lawyers who registered for the course to have a strong reputation in the field.

3. The lawyers believed the course would both be enjoyable and informative and contribute to the lawyer's meeting the needs of the lawyer's clients and/or the lawyer's firm.

4. The course would assist the lawyer and the law firm in moving into a new area of practice or expanding the legal services in areas where the firm already provided some legal services.

5. The course would help improve the operations of the law firm (or government agency or in-house counsel situation) where the lawyer works.

These explicit reasons why lawyers register for a course create the analytical framework for determining whether a business case can be made for any new subject to be offered in the continuing legal education marketplace. The analysis below shows why a strong business case can be made that bar associations and private continuing legal education providers should begin offering leadership development courses for lawyers and persons who work in legal organizations.

Leadership development education in the United States, Europe, and Australia has become quite "mature" as a discipline with courses taught in universities, colleges, community colleges, high schools, professional continuing education courses, custom-built courses delivered in major companies and professional service organizations, and other graduate schools and postsecondary institutions. There are textbooks on leadership theory and practice, leadership skills development workbooks and courses on leadership development that generate an estimated $2 billion in tuition revenue. Leadership development courses are required in Master of Business Administration (MBA) programs and in other graduate programs across the United States.

Because lawyers are called upon to lead as an integral part of the professional work they provide as leaders of their firms and staffs, and in the professional services they provide to clients, a course on leadership development for lawyers meets the first prong of the test posed in our analytical framework. A leadership development course would be considered "timely," and the content/information would be of "critical importance" to a significant number of lawyers. We will return to the second prong of the test after reviewing the others.

The third prong of the test cited above, that lawyers believed the course would both be enjoyable and informative and contribute to the lawyer's meeting the needs of the lawyer's clients and/or the lawyer's firm, can also be met by a course on leadership development for lawyers. As shown throughout this book, leadership development courses help the lawyer improve the services provided by the lawyer.

Lawyers as counselors and advocates must lead, even though they are the agent in the principal/agency client/lawyer relationship. Lawyers have specialized knowledge and generalized experience that give them the ability to give their clients sound advice worth hundreds of dollars per hour. Being a better leader is one of the skill improvement areas that will surely help lawyers improve the services they provide to their clients.

The fourth prong of the test cited above is that lawyers choose a course because they believe it could help them expand the services provided by the lawyer or the law firm. This prong is also met by this type of course. Being a better, more reflective and knowledgeable leader and receiving specific training in the area of leadership development can open up new possibilities for work as their clients become aware they have completed leadership development courses. Lawyers who have taken leadership development courses will be called upon to provide a broader range of legal services, asked to accept more leadership roles with their clients, and asked to provide more leadership-oriented advice.

The fifth prong, that lawyers choose courses that they believe will help improve the operations of the law firm or government agency or in-house counsel situation where they work, can also be met by a course on leadership development. This prong is especially important because leadership development courses for lawyers can be developed in a generic mode and taught as one-day or multiday seminars, or they can be custom designed to work with specific law firms, government agencies and in-house counsel situations. Custom-designed leadership training would require research into each specific organization receiving the training and the development of specific leadership development training to address current challenges and expected challenges of the organization. Such leadership development training can be of varying lengths and could be designed to secure continuing legal education credit for the participants and yet be specialized enough to contribute greatly to improvement in the leadership and operations of the law firm, government agency, or in-house counsel situation.

Thus, four of the five prongs of the tests that lawyers use to choose CLE courses can be met by leadership development courses. The second prong regarding what lawyers look for in deciding to take a CLE course—that the CLE sponsor and CLE seminar leader have a strong reputation in the field—is admittedly missing. Because no such courses have been offered, no CLE seminar leader stands out in the field and no CLE sponsor has experience in offering such a course. However, there are good seminar leaders in the leadership development field, and there are good CLE sponsors with excellent reputations. For lawyers to know that the seminar leader has a strong reputation, that seminar leader will need to have delivered several excellent leadership development courses before that reputation becomes solid. Thus, although there is an important element missing in the business case analysis, the first mover, the first CLE sponsor and seminar leader who join forces to put on an excellent leadership development course, will gain the benefit of solidifying their reputations, and others who come into the marketplace after them will have a more difficult time capturing some of the reputation or market space from the first mover.

Since leadership development courses will assist lawyers in being more professional, they should be awarded CLE credit. For a course to obtain CLE credit, the course must be approved by the continuing legal education board of each state that requires CLE attendance by each lawyer. We believe the time is now right for this to occur in every state. Thus, a strong business case can be made for CLE administrators to work with potential vendors to develop courses on leadership development for lawyers for CLE credit.

Over time, one might create specialized leadership development courses for judges, litigators, and mediators, and leadership courses could be refined to target certain types of attorneys, including business law, intellectual property lawyers, criminal defense attorneys, real estate lawyers, and other practice areas.

Leadership development courses will also help the legal profession to deal more effectively with an important development in the history of the legal profession: the emergence of women in leadership positions in law firms and legal organizations. It is now imperative that the legal profession better understand how to promote and accommodate the future growing presence of women in leadership positions in legal organizations. Chapter 6 addresses this topic squarely and is based on new research, interviews, and surveys of women who have achieved leadership positions in the legal profession.

CHAPTER SIX
WOMEN, LEADERSHIP, AND THE LAW

By Laura Rothacker

The role of women in the legal profession is at a crossroads. The disparity between the large number of women in the profession and the small number of women who occupy positions of authority in the legal profession is analogous to the huge role black athletes play in professional sports and the limited role they play in positions of authority in professional sports. The experiences of the primary author of this chapter, an attorney who commenced her career as one of the first women attorneys serving as in-house counsel in a large insurance company and who later became a senior partner in one of the largest law firms in Denver, were essential to gathering the information necessary to write this chapter and putting all of this information into context. This is a chapter written about women by a woman who has been there and is dedicated to improving both the legal profession and the role of women in it.

The legal profession is at the forefront in implementing change for society and business. It is a dynamic profession that attracts bright, competitive young people, many of whom highly value fairness and equality. Women currently constitute over 50 percent of the law students graduating from law schools, but represent a significantly smaller percentage of partners in large law firms, tenured professors at law schools, judges, and lawmakers around the country. In this chapter we explore systemic issues that contribute to the shortage of women in leadership positions in the legal profession. In addition to a review of the literature on women in the legal profession, we surveyed women lawyers to elicit information regarding the current status of women in leadership positions and the differences in leadership styles between male and female attorneys.

The first woman admitted to a State Bar (Iowa) in 1869 saw her quest to become a lawyer foiled by the United States Supreme Court in a decision in 1873 that declared women "unfit for the law."[14] Arabella Mansfield was the first of a long line of women who were denied admission to practice law in various states and were even denied admission to law schools on a regular basis during the late 1800s and early 1900s.

Women did persist in their pursuit of law degrees and admission to the male dominated elite who comprised the legal profession. Ada Kepley received her law degree in Illinois in 1870 and Charlotte Ray, an African American women, received her law degree in 1872 from Howard University.[15] These women paved the way for the progress in the profession that we will document in this chapter and that this chapter is also designed to promote as we have far to go until the day that women reach an appropriate level of leadership positions in the legal profession.

Until the period between the 1960s and early 1970s many law schools strictly limited the admission of women to a few token numbers, if any. This changed with the passage of Title IX in 1975, which was not implemented by most schools until the mid to late '70s. The purpose of Title IX was to provide women with equal access to education. In 1978, a date well-remembered by this author, the raging debate at many law schools was whether law firms that had a stated policy that male law students were to be interviewed for associate positions and female law students were to be interviewed only for legal secretary positions should be banned from conducting interviews. Such blatant sexual discrimination was not only absurd in 2005, it was especially absurd for a profession that prides itself as being a leader in promoting fairness and equality in our society.

Women practicing law prior to 1985 faced significant overt discrimination in this male dominated profession. In order to understand the current issues facing women as they aspire to leadership positions in the legal profession, it is important to acknowledge that much has changed for the better over the past twenty years and that the now prevalent barriers to women in the legal profession are less severe and obvious. Yet, in spite of this prog-

---

14 Drachman, Virginia G., *Women Lawyers and the Origins of Professional Identity in American: The Letters of the Equity Club, 1887 to 1890* (Ann Arbor: University of Michigan Press, 1993).
15 Ibid.

ress, there remain systemic issues prevalent in society, as well as in the legal profession, that act to preclude women from significant leadership positions.

In the 1900s, the predominant style of leadership and advocacy in the male-dominated legal profession was one of control and subordination. The central characteristic of this leadership style was a top-down command style that controlled subordinates through aggressive dominance.[16] A woman emerging from law school prior to the mid-1980s was torn between either adopting the prevailing male-oriented style of leadership or trying to deploy her own predominant, more female-oriented style of leadership—which typically emphasized teamwork and sharing of both responsibility and credit. Often women's efforts failed regardless which route they chose. If a female attorney adopted a command and control style of leadership, she was perceived as (and often referred to as) a "dragon lady" or worse. If she sought to instill a more collaborative style of leadership, she was perceived (and labelled) as weak and ineffectual by many of her more senior male colleagues.

As the number of women in the legal profession grew during the 1970s and 1980s, women lawyers were expected by male senior partners to emulate men in all outward respects if they wanted to rise to leadership in the firm or legal organization. Many women during this period dressed like men in dark suits with silk bow ties, little makeup, and "sensible" shoes. Women began to use sports metaphors, patiently listened to sexually explicit and frequently offensive jokes by male counterparts in the legal profession, and basically pretended or fervently hoped that the gender barriers to entry and leadership would go away once they "proved themselves."

In greater and greater numbers since 1970, women did prove themselves in the legal profession. As a result, much of the overt discrimination has disappeared. Unfortunately, in large part it was not due to the mentoring and guidance of the male senior members of firms that made this possible. It was the dedication, loyalty,

---

16 We acknowledge this chapter includes reference to "male" and "female" predominant styles of leadership which could be viewed as "stereotypes." We acknowledge that these, like all generalizations, never perfectly represent reality. However, our research has shown these constructs are both valid and illuminative and are necessary to depict past and current plight of women in the legal profession.

and praise for women lawyers from clients using the legal services of women attorneys that made men in the legal profession realize that women could be very successful lawyers as well as strong leaders in the profession.

The success of women and the support of their clients in both the legal and business worlds permitted women to achieve a significant measure of freedom from the authoritarian leadership style of the male-dominated profession. In many cases when women became partners in firms, it was because they both adapted male stereotypes of behavior and had the strong vocal support of their clients. As the evolution of women in the legal workplace began to take hold in the 1980s, many women, when they became partners, began to liberate themselves from the need to act "like the men." This courageous act freed those women from the outward requirements of male-oriented appearance and style. Thanks in part to Anita Hill, sexually offensive behaviors have become more limited and are, in the legal profession as a whole, now the exception and not the rule.

With the growing professional success of women throughout the 1970s, 1980s, and 1990s and the enormous increase in the number of women attending law schools and graduating at or near the top of their classes, one would reasonably have expected a commensurate increase in the number of women rising to take over in traditional leadership roles in the legal profession. This was not the case during this period, and it is not the case today. Although there are many strong women in leadership positions in the legal profession, the numbers are not statistically representative of the aggregate number of women who are practicing law. We must now explore some of the reasons that we have observed from experience regarding why women are not reaching the top of the profession of law even in 2006.

Collaborative Leadership

The old style of leadership both in business and law, and as most recently exhibited by our fellow attorney, John R. Bolton, is the "kiss up and kick down" form of leadership. It exercises reverence to autocratic rulers ("kiss up") and contentious dominance over ("kick down") subordinates. This style of leadership has proven to be shortsighted for those who want to lead in an empowering, ethical, and effective manner. In 2005, this style of leadership was flatly rejected by the U.S. Senate in refusing to confirm Bolton's nomination as Ambassador of the United Nations.

Most academic treatises on leadership and scholars of leadership development suggest that a new style of leadership will be more effective in a world of diverse populations and rapidly changing paradigms. This style of leadership is called collaborative or transformational leadership. Collaborative leadership persuades, empowers, and partners with others as a team to achieve a goal. Transformational leadership, as espoused by Burns and others, cites the key role of leaders as helping their followers become leaders themselves as a direct result of their participation in the leadership activities designed by leaders. The role of the collaborative leader or transformational leader is to enhance and maximize the skills and contribution of each team member in order to create the best result. The collaborative leader is responsible for keeping the team operating efficiently and staying on task. The collaborative or transformational leader is responsible for making sure that all followers are given the resources they need to be effective. Collaborative leaders take primary responsibility for resolving and heading off all major conflicts within the group. Collaborative leaders actively create opportunities for subordinates and followers to grow and mature to transform into leaders in their own right.

Both research and the experiential data collected by women leaders document the fact that women often excel as collaborative leaders. In comprehensive studies of senior men and women executives conducted by Robert Kabacoff, Ph.D., of the Management Research Group, senior women executives were rated by peers, bosses, and independently as:

- Having a greater degree of energy, intensity, and emotional expression

- Having a greater capacity to keep others enthusiastic and involved

- More likely to set deadlines and monitor progress to ensure the completion of activities

- Setting higher expectations for performance for both themselves and others

The implications of these findings cannot be exaggerated. When the leadership style of the legal profession shifts from command and control to collaborative leadership, as we predict it will over the next decade, women in the legal profession will be uniquely poised to take advantage of the change in the leadership culture. We predict that at rates unprecedented in previous history women will rise to levels of leadership that statisticians would predict given their increasing numbers and their excellent rankings in law schools. And, as more and more women succeed in reaching leadership positions in the general business world, one can be assured that many of these women business leaders will seek out and hire women attorneys who share their values and leadership styles.

Certainly, many men can be and are excellent collaborative leaders. Yet, it is not too great a generalization to state that experience has shown and still shows that men in the legal profession, be they associates or managing partners, are frequently steered or mentored toward the old-fashioned, more masculine command and control styles of leadership. We have seen a few select male senior partners of both large and small firms who consistently use and teach collaborative leadership. These men, the exceptions to the rule, regularly choose the best attorneys (men and women) for projects based upon their expertise and give them significant authority over their part of the transaction. They solicit and take the advice of others who work on their legal teams. They include the client as an integral part of the decision-making team. They practice inclusive leadership, getting the best from all who participate on the team. Lawyers who practice collaborative leadership make sure that they do not take an autocratic role in the transaction. They excel at being facilitators, mediators, and consummate litigators or deal makers. They create a loyal client base and associates who in turn grow in their own leadership capabilities. Collaborative leaders are those in the legal profession who are helping to pave the way for women to become leaders in the legal profession in the future. Our experience suggests that they are growing in number in the profession, though we could not find any research specifically on this aspect of leadership in the legal profession.

Based upon our own experiences and the professional success and skills of the thousands of women both in and entering the legal profession, it is clear that as the shift toward collaborative leadership takes hold the strong competencies that many women lawyers possess will assist them in moving quickly and successfully forward as leaders in the legal profession in private firms, corporations, and government agencies. Now, we explore contributing factors currently holding many women back and keeping them from reaching the top tier of leadership positions in the profession today. Although these barriers do exist, they are in fact artificial or contrived, as will be documented below.

Barriers to Women Achieving Leadership Roles in the Legal Profession

Women experience many artificial barriers to leadership in the legal profession. Many of the barriers are ingrained in the fabric of the daily work environment and society and some of the barriers are imposed by women on themselves. The barriers identified through our research include:

- The "quicksand problem"
- Mommy track
- Compensation, networking, and business development structures
- Gender differences related to motivational factors
- Gender differences in communication and the setting of expectations

Many women lawyers have proven to be effective at juggling conflicting demands on their time. Notwithstanding that skill, many women often demand perfection of themselves in every endeavor they undertake. Thus, if they believe they cannot do a job to their own high level of expectation, they will not ever undertake it. Stephanie Pincus, M.D., a former senior-level executive of the Veterans Administration, calls this the "quicksand problem." The more women struggle to be the perfect lawyer, the perfect mother, the perfect wife, the perfect daughter, and perfect community supporter, the quicker she falls out of the game completely when one or more of these endeavors is not performed at the level of expertise and perfection to which she is accustomed to and demands of herself.

We have observed that, unlike many women, many men who aspire to or succeed in undertaking leadership roles in the legal profession create a shift in their lives to accommodate the excessive time demands and rigorous physical and intellectual demands that such leadership roles now require in the legal profession. Many men make sure that their other roles (father, husband, son, community contributor, etc.) are quickly downgraded in importance and effort to accommodate their ambition to achieve a leadership role in their law firm, legal organization, and the legal profession itself. Less attention or quality effort is devoted to these other endeavors early in the march to leadership positions in the legal profession. That is, in part, made possible by the fact that in society men are viewed (by both men and women) to have "lesser" responsibility for family, community, and home. The primary responsibility for the maintenance and well-being of family, home, and community continues to fall more heavily on women. These attitudes may slowly shift in time, but clearly the near future does not suggest any significant change in this area.

This differential in the roles of men and women in the home, community, and family creates a very challenging dynamic between men and women attorneys in the work environment. Some men who lament when they miss their child's birthday party or their child's surgery because they had to be on a conference call or at a deposition wear the sacrifice as a badge of honor. It is also viewed as such by many senior male attorneys. Implicitly, male-dominated law firms use this type of situation as an example to be emulated by those who "want to get to the top." On the other hand, many women attorneys wear their failure to meet their children's needs as they perceive them as a badge of dishonor, many suffering extreme guilt, leading to unhappiness, decreased productivity, and in some cases due to the "quicksand trap,"[17] leaving the practice of law all together at a fairly early age, never to return. Trying to balance the desire to be "perfect" against the demands of work and family is extremely difficult. The superwoman myth is just that, a myth.

---

17 We use the quicksand metaphor because legend has it that when a person falls into an area we call quicksand it is often the case that the harder that they fight and struggle to stay afloat the quicker they fall below the surface and expire.

One example of how a family has balanced its work responsibilities and allowed a woman to reach the pinnacle of leadership in her law firm and in her community is the example of the primary author of this chapter. Laura Rothacker's husband is a business executive. Laura and her husband have a blended family of five children. During their busy careers, the husband and the wife both needed a "wife at home." In this situation, and it is a situation that will be repeated more and more over time, it was the husband, and not the wife, who stayed at home with the children more often than not.

Women need to recognize the quicksand problem very early in their careers. They need to create a home life and allocation of familial duties that allows them the time and energy to take on leadership responsibilities in the legal profession. Improving the leadership skills and delegation skills of women is an additional approach that can assist women in striking a sustainable balance between work and family that sacrifices neither their opportunities to obtain leadership positions in the field of law nor the needs and the demands of their families. Women need to assert that they can be leaders in the legal profession. Then, and only then, will they be accorded the flexibility both in their home lives and in their law firms to lead in a manner that they determine is most effective to get the job done both at home and at work.

Another key strategy for women to deploy to be more successful as leaders is to form support groups in the legal profession. These support groups could be composed of both men and women and could serve as an invaluable resource for mentoring, guidance and advice, and outright support and assistance in times of emergencies or great need. In addition to support groups, women in the legal profession could help their rise to leadership positions by writing more articles, giving speeches, and taking a public stand that women with significant family responsibilities can and will be among the best people to become leaders in the legal profession and in their communities.

Women lawyers who are significantly involved in their community can act as effective bridges between the legal profession and the community, bridges that are badly needed as our society becomes more fragmented. Although family and the law often take up 110 percent of the time for many women, holding community positions as members of boards of directors or advisors to organizations can pay huge dividends in terms of client development, name recognition, and gaining the respect of peers and superiors in the legal profession.

Some efforts on the part of law firms to "accommodate women" have actually limited the leadership opportunities of women. Many firms have created a de facto "mommy track." Firms have by and large complied with the Family and Medical Leave Act, but, by creating a mommy track these firms, intentionally or not, actually relegate mothers to second-class citizenship in the law firm or legal organization. Women "afforded" mommy track status universally earn lower financial rewards than their male counterparts (and former classmates) due to fewer billable hours. Even worse, the best clients and matters in the firm or legal organization are systematically steered away from them. The result is almost always the same: women lawyers on the mommy track are rarely appointed to management committees or become leaders in their firms. In many firms the mommy track is also synonymous with being a "nonequity" partner. Often, when women take time to care for their children or families, it is interpreted as a lack of commitment to the firm and often an abdication of their responsibilities to the firm, their clients, and the profession as a whole. Abdication is not a route to leadership in any endeavor, but fulfilling multiple roles is not an abdication, nor is it a voluntary decision to drop to second-class status within the firm or the profession.

The needs of women to balance work and family priorities may require that leadership roles for some women simply be delayed for some time, not that they become unattainable when the woman can and is willing to again devote extensive hours to the firm. The needs of children and families differ, and there may be times when professional leadership roles need to take a backseat, but such leadership roles must not be permanently barred to women who cannot accept them while family demands are at their peak. A well thought-out long-term view of the contributions that women can make to the law firm, legal organization, and the legal profession over time is needed so that women who prefer not to have positions of leadership during their child bearing years will not be "overlooked" for leadership responsibilities during their most professionally productive years, which may be in their 40s, 50s, or 60s.

Another artificial barrier that exists to women reaching leadership roles in law firms and legal organizations is the concept of aggregate billable hours. The business world is changing so rapidly that old expectations have gone by the wayside. Clients have embraced the flexibility made possible by technology. Using technology so that it becomes a benefit rather than a burden through effective leadership is best demonstrated by those who understand that every minute is valuable time. It takes leadership to eliminate unnecessary meetings, conference calls, electronic mail messages, and general busy work even though it cuts back on billable hours and for those firms that bill this way cuts back on gross revenues. Unfortunately, efficiency is not always highly regarded or rewarded in the legal profession. A conference call, meeting research, and legal drafting are most often billed on an hourly basis whether they were important or not. Some clients are trying to change this paradigm by placing "caps" on fees for single projects or cases or paying flat-rate monthly retainers or project fees. The drive to cap fees has created one type of situation that is not beneficial for the client. Law firms with caps on legal fees often decide to deploy cheaper, less skilled, subordinates to perform more of the work required by clients. Although the total price may go down, the total number of hours devoted to a task or project remains stays the same or even increases. The quality of work may be comparable, but in many cases it deteriorates, because experienced attorneys are taken off the matter. Experienced, highly skilled women lawyers often lose out under this approach, as do clients.

At the same time, billable hours demanded of associates have risen dramatically over the past decade. The economics of the matter are simple and straightforward. The more hours per attorney billed and collected by the firm, the greater the firm's gross and net revenues. The current norm in large metropolitan areas is 2,000 to 2,200 billable hours per year or higher. In the 1970s it was 1,600 to 1,800 hours. The current expectation of 2,000 or more billable hours works to the significant disadvantage of any attorney, man or woman, who has substantial family or other responsibilities outside of the workplace. Again, this development has had a strong negative impact on women in the legal profession.

Attorneys who have juggled, or expect to juggle, family responsibilities and their legal careers must now step forward to become collaborative leaders who create and win approval of methods for achieving both excellence for their clients and a productive, flexible place for attorneys to work. Women should be aware of how this billable hour focus of the legal profession is an institutional form of discrimination against their achieving success and obtaining leadership roles. Other professions have found ways to link results and success to promoting people to leadership positions and to reward efficiency and effectiveness over simple measures of billable hours or aggregate time. Money, power, and leadership are inextricably linked in our society. As long as the current system links billable hours to compensation and eventual leadership roles in the firm, attorneys who have family responsibilities are at a great disadvantage, even when they are more efficient, more effective and more productive for their clients than their counterparts. The pressure for billable hours is less entrenched in both government agencies and in-house counsel offices. Larger numbers of women have succeeded in these formats, but still not at statistically representative levels. More research needs to be undertaken to find the root causes of why women are not at the forefront of these organizations in numbers proportionate to their skills and experience. There could be a myriad of reasons, including the fact that corporate transfers, reductions in force, and mergers may take a higher toll on younger, less tenured employees, many of whom are female or who, as wives and mothers, have less flexibility to transfer from city to city to take advantage of the best career opportunities offered to lawyers in government or corporate offices.

Being a caring, involved parent does not preclude obtaining leadership position in the legal professions. Women need to mentor and be supportive of other women and men who have significant family responsibilities and encourage them to undertake leadership roles and act as leaders for others with similar concerns. Creating a strong, informal support system that goes beyond the office can make the difference between success and failure for many women. In addition to their obvious practical benefits, such support systems create a sense of security that permits women with home and client obligations to take on additional responsibilities that they may otherwise refuse to take, but for the knowledge that they had a safety net. If a woman knows that there are people she trusts to step in and assist her in an emergency, or when conflicting demands of home and work become too great, then she will be much more likely to undertake tasks that she may be otherwise reluctant to attempt. Strong, compassionate collaborative leaders are needed to instruct the legal profession in how to balance (or juggle) the multitude of demands placed upon women both inside and outside the legal profession.

Unfortunately, the stress and demand of balancing career and family has caused many casualties or dropouts from the legal profession among our best and brightest women attorneys. The additional energy it takes to fight the system and attempt to create a workplace that is conducive and supportive to women undergoing dual careers of law and motherhood has and continues to cause many women to drop out of the legal profession entirely. Any profession that consistently has women leave because of "family demands" should assume that it is not the family that is pulling these women away, but the work environment that is driving them away. This represents a waste of great human capital that drops directly to the bottom line of legal organizations and the profession as a whole. Changing perspectives and methods deeply imbedded in the legal profession can result in the changes needed in the culture and practice to promote the appropriate level of success of women. As stated elsewhere in this book, because the legal profession is currently experiencing significant challenges, it is integral to the long-term success of the profession that increased meaningful participation by women in leadership positions be encouraged and supported in order to help find real solutions to many of the problems the profession is currently facing.

An additional artificial barrier to women preventing them from achieving leadership positions is the client development and compensation systems employed in the legal profession. Traditional client development and compensation systems in the legal profession discriminate against women. They may not intentionally discriminate, but they clearly and systematically discriminate, nonetheless in several key ways. First, bringing in the client is deemed more important than keeping the client in most compensation formulas used by law firms. Most of the reward systems in private firms reward the "rainmaker" more than the "lead attorney" who does most of the work on the case. It is clear that bringing the client through the door is important, but keeping the client and doing excellent work for the client are equally important. A maxim of the real estate industry is that it is far more expensive to replace a tenant than it is to keep one. The same applies in law, but most firms place far greater weight on bringing in the client that doing the good work to keep the client. Women often excel at creating supportive, long-term relationships of trust with clients. It takes time to achieve this, but once achieved it is a bond that few clients are willing to or feel the necessity to break. Over several years these relationships can become client generation vehicles as clients move from business to business or rise themselves in the hierarchy in the business or client organization. If the firm structure is such that these long-term relationships are not valued or rewarded as much as bringing in the client, then women will fall behind their more rapid-fire client-generating male counterparts. This has and will continue to result in women leaving the profession or leaving a particular firm and finding other avenues or places for their time and talents. They simply drop out of what they perceive as a rat race where men have many structural advantages.

Firms must recognize that many clients are loyal to the attorney and not the firm. If senior women associates or partners leave law firms and go to other firms, the firm the female lawyer has left is at risk of losing significant clients that it has served. This in the long run not only hurts the bottom line and reputation of the firm, it forces the firm that has just lost some key clients when women leave to stoke the client development fire at even greater heat levels, thereby causing the firm to place even greater emphasis and greater rewards on obtaining new clients. The cycle gets repeated to the greater detriment of the women who remain at the firm after one or more women attorneys leave the firm and take key clients with them.

Another artificial client development and professional barrier women face is that traditional out-of-office networking and client development activities used by law firms to generate new business (and paid for handsomely by law firms) are designed, either consciously or unconsciously, by men for men, giving them a huge institutional advantage over women in the firm. Most women, due to family commitments and lack of interest in sports, cannot or do not afford spend the time it takes to play golf or attend professional sporting events paid for by law firms to help their male attorneys obtain new clients. Some women simply do not have the background or interest in sports or golf to bring a meaningful level of banter to the sports networking event to be effective at client generation in these venues. Over time, the legal profession must realize that being a leader in the profession should not require that women take up golf or become an expert at professional sports, unless they are so inclined. Although some men who are senior partners might respond, "Well, that's what works in bringing in clients," to justify the skyboxes and season ticket prices that are now astronomical, some law firms have become quite creative and successful in promoting client development and networking events that are much better suited to the style and culture of women lawyers.

To address the bias in client development activities senior women attorneys at several firms around the country have created women's oriented client development and networking events. The senior women partners in one firm embarked on this venture by inviting women clients, women business leaders, and women community leaders to a cocktail party, with the announced intention of providing a place where women could network with other women they may not otherwise encounter in their day-to-day careers. (Law firms are uniquely situated to do this because their client base usually stretches across many professional areas.) The initial event had approximately 50 women attending, including the women from the host law firm. These events grew over time to include over 350 women attendees. From these events the firm learned that women in the business community (the potential clients) are as strapped for time as women lawyers. Most women business leaders would prefer to spend an hour at a cocktail party networking than three to six hours at a golf course or professional sporting event with their lawyers or potential lawyer.

These types of networking events and client development activities designed by women lawyers for women lawyers give women the opportunity to cultivate relationships that down the road will create the longstanding, personally and financially rewarding client relationships they desire. As more and more women become leaders in business, the opportunities and effectiveness of women lawyers as client developers will increase substantially. Many women in business are not quick to chose a lawyer or law firm. They will not often select a lawyer or law firm based upon one meeting or one networking event. A short networking event opens the door for women attorneys to introduce themselves to potential clients in a mutually comfortable, time-sensitive, and rewarding setting. Thereafter, for the female potential client to become a client of the firm, it will often require a commitment by the women attorney to earn the respect and trust of the potential client. These nontraditional forms of networking and client development need to be supported by law firms both financially and professionally to promote equality between women and men in seeking new business for the firm. Client development events and their hefty budgets that are clearly biased toward mega sporting events not only discriminate against attorneys with substantial family responsibilities, they discriminate against women in the business community as well. This discrimination is finally now starting to be noticed by many in the legal profession, although it has been noticed by women in the legal profession for decades. In the long run the firms that are creative in designing and supporting client development events that work well for each gender on an equal, fair basis will be the most successful for the law firm and the women attorneys in the firm.

When firms require specific amounts of new client generation by attorneys who are trying to balance the demands of partnership with the demands of a young family, those attorneys will either be shuttled into lesser positions or leave the firm out of frustration. It may well take women attorneys longer to generate business. Firms need to be patient in this regard and not further handicap women by removing them from consideration for leadership positions simply because their client generation results do not match the early results of young male associates or junior partners. Given time and support, the financial benefit to the firm from client retention and generation by women can be dramatic and substantial. Firms that are shortsighted will not only lose the legal talents of women attorneys, but lose some of their potential client base as well as excellent women attorneys begin to leave to join more gender friendly and progressive law firms.

Removing artificial barriers in compensation, networking, client development practices, mentoring, and leadership must be coupled with an understanding of gender-based differences in what motivates men and women and how they communicate. Often, for competitive men their income level becomes the measure of their accomplishments against others, and, in turn, is directly related to their self-esteem and workplace satisfaction. The men in many law firms are very aware of what every other attorney makes and how many hours each bills and collects. If a man or woman with whom he feels is an equal is rewarded at a higher level, he often threatens to leave the firm or in fact may leave the firm. For most women, income is a factor, but not the sole determinate of their self-worth, nor such a strong component of their workplace satisfaction level. Women lawyers report that they work for a variety of reasons, including intellectual stimulation, plus a full range of rewards including income, a desire to help others, and a sense of achievement.

In addition men, to a much greater extent than women in the legal profession, have a well-defined and well-accepted culture of self-promotion. Gender-based expectations of society do not penalize men for aggressively acting in their own self-interest. Conversely, both in society, and especially in the legal profession, many women who act aggressively in their own self-interest often become suspect or not trusted or well regarded by their peers and their superiors. This double standard may not be intentional or conscious. For that reason, it will likely be hard to dislodge it in the legal profession or in society as a whole.

Women in most societies, including our own, often tend to understate their achievements. "Smart" girls are taught even today that they can succeed in school and still be "nice" (read modest, sweet, humble, and feminine). The real world, especially the competitive legal world, does not reward humble or sweet behavior or personalities. Women lawyers are thus constantly torn between showing humility and showcasing their own accomplishments. In an ideal world they expect their peers and colleagues to know and acknowledge their achievements and to reward them appropriately and fairly. It is not an ideal world. The disinclination of professional women in business, and especially in law, to promote themselves aggressively, combined with the negative reactions from their colleagues when they do, has had far-reaching negative consequences, including a pattern of discrimination against women when women are reviewed by their male superiors in the legal profession for promotion or setting their compensation level. This should be addressed by having both genders included in the leadership selection process and compensation decisions in more than token roles and these issues are brought to the forefront of promotion decision-making processes.

The full potential for women to obtain and excel at leadership positions in the legal profession can be accomplished, however, only if the changes we describe take place and if women simultaneously overcome their reluctance to self-promote and aggressively and continually seek positions of leadership. When women in the legal profession act in a subordinate manner, they will get walked on. Therefore, legal organizations must create venues for women to showcase their accomplishments without negative consequences arising from prejudices against "pushy women." All of these changes will not come about overnight. They will require hard work and leadership training. Only then will we be able to maximize the potential contributions of every member of the legal profession. That is the goal of this chapter.

The positive effects of seeking and receiving acknowledgment and recognition have been the subject of recent studies applicable to the current fate of women in the legal profession today. The book *Necessary Dreams: The Role of Ambition in Women's Lives*, by Dr. Anna Fels, a psychiatrist, makes the cogent argument that seeking and receiving acknowledgment and recognition are essential sources of energy that propels people to become and remain leaders.[18] Dr. Fels suggests that by minimizing their own accomplishments and failing to seek recognition, acknowledgment, and rewards aggressively for their accomplishments, women are cutting off their energy and ability to achieve leadership positions and succeed in those positions over the long run.

Younger women attorneys have less of an expectation of discrimination and are thus more likely to become frustrated and angry when they encounter what they perceive as unfair treatment. Without strong leadership and mentoring they will be more likely to seek other positions or to drop out of the profession entirely rather than fight to correct the challenges women face in the profession. This will exacerbate the problem. That is why it is imperative that steps be taken to help the legal profession appropriately mine the talents of the many highly skilled women

---

18 Fels, Dr. Anna. *Necessary Dreams: Ambition in Changing Women's Lives.* HARVARD BUSINESS BOOKS (Boston, 2004).

graduating from law schools today, tomorrow, and over the past three decades.

Conclusion

Riane Eisler, a social scientist and attorney, states in the article "Economics of the Enlightened Use of Power," "There are obvious differences between men and women, but much that is considered masculine and feminine is our heritage from earlier times when women were barred from positions of leadership and power."[19] Time alone will not correct the imbalances. Women must compete for leadership in the legal profession, or they will remain disproportionately disenfranchised and marginalized in a profession where they will become a majority in our lifetime. Women must actively support each other and support men who are attempting to remove artificial barriers to women achieving leadership positions in the profession. As more and more women enter business and law, enlightened and effective leaders, regardless of gender, will require that these issues be addressed. Those leaders in the legal profession that find a means to support both men and women in becoming and succeeding as leaders will become the most successful leaders in a competitive legal world that demands expertise, hard work, creativity, and ethics. This chapter addresses a small, but important, number of the many issues attendant to "Women, Leadership, and the Law." It is one part of a national effort to bring the best that the leadership literature and leadership development practices have to offer a profession that has a long history of leading the country with regard to issues of fairness and equality and that has shown the ability to grow and evolve. The goal of the legal profession must be to maximize the contributions of all of its members. Neither men nor women in the legal profession can afford to permit differences in style, roles, communication, compensation, or client development practices to continue to undermine the efforts of future women leaders to serve their clients, their law firms, their communities, their families, and our worthy profession.

---

19 *Enlightened Power: How Women Are Transforming the Practice of Leadership,* by Linda Coughlin, Ellen Wingard, Keith Hollihan, eds. JOSEY-BASS (San Francisco, 2005).

CHAPTER SEVEN
THE VALUE OF LEADERSHIP DEVELOPMENT IN THE PROFESSION

If leadership development training merely answered Judge Barr's question in the affirmative, by helping lawyers become better lawyers, that would be enough to justify the expenditure of significant sums on this effort. But before we expect anyone to spend money on leadership development for lawyers, this chapter attempts to provide evidence and a rationale why leadership development programs can create significant value in the legal profession as a whole. Significant problems that are currently being experienced in the legal profession were listed earlier in this book:

- High rates of dissatisfaction among young attorneys
- Poor reputation of lawyers within the society
- High departure rate for trained, qualified, and certified lawyers from the legal profession
- Growing economic pressures on law firms of all sizes, especially large firms
- High levels of client dissatisfaction and formal complaints and malpractice actions against lawyers
- Growing levels of associate turnover
- Prevalence of outdated governance practices at many law firms
- Continuing evidence of a glass ceiling for women in law firms
- Client challenges to paying increasingly large legal bills and insistence on alternative billing structures
- Growing numbers of ethical complaints against lawyers

- Increasing competition and growing use of questionable means to obtain clients/business

- Increasing lack of civility among lawyers

- Increasing delays in litigation, arbitration, and even mediation

- Lack of training in leadership in a profession whose members lead clients, lead organizations, serve on boards of directors, and hold high political and governmental positions, all without the benefit of the knowledge created in the field of leadership during the past fifty years

We take each one of these items and discuss how leadership development courses for lawyers can assist individual lawyers, firms, in-house counsel, and government lawyers in addressing them.

High rates of dissatisfaction among young attorneys

One recent book has been entirely devoted to this topic: *How Lawyers Lose Their Way: A Profession Fails Its Creative Minds*, by Jean Stefancic and Richard Delgado.[20] This book argues that formalism and the pursuit of profit at the expense of ethics is behind much of the dissatisfaction lawyers experience. These authors present a compelling argument that there is something terribly wrong in the legal profession today. The authors state, "... thousands more [lawyers] would benefit if their lives contained more leisure, more contemplation, more time to think seriously about what they do, and even, enjoy it."[21] Further support for the thesis that lawyers are dissatisfied and something can be done about it can be found in law review articles such as "Why Lawyers Are Unhappy" by Martin E.P. Seligman, Paul R. Verkuil, and Terry H. Kang.[22]

---

20 Jean Stefancic and Richard Delgado, *How Lawyers Lose Their Way: A Profession Fails Its Creative Minds* (Durham: Duke University Press, 2005).
21 Ibid., 84.
22 Martin E.P. Seligman, Paul R. Verkuil, and Terry H. Kang, "Why Lawyers Are Unhappy," *Cardozo Law Review* 23 (2001): 33.

THE VALUE OF LEADERSHIP DEVELOPMENT IN THE PROFESSION

Leadership development courses can address this very high level of dissatisfaction among lawyers. Teaching and learning leadership development skills and aptitudes requires self-examination, introspection, getting to know oneself better, and becoming clearer regarding one's own goals and values. It requires getting out of the law office, away from the minute-by-minute pressures of client demands and hourly billing quotas. It requires not only studying leadership theory and practice, but also looking at biographies that show how others rose to leadership, found their calling, and learned to contribute to society. Leadership development courses can help people empower themselves, energizing them, and put them on a path to make a unique mark on society and the people and organizations they serve.

The study of leadership development theory and practice by lawyers, of course, cannot guarantee great new insights, new approaches, and behaviors that generate lasting satisfaction among lawyers. Leadership development courses by themselves cannot ease the economic pressures that lawyers face and the daily challenges of dealing with clients with whom a lawyer may not agree or whose goals the lawyer cannot personally embrace. The study of leadership development can, however, guarantee to the lawyer and those who work in the legal profession the opening of new avenues to approach the daily grind of being a lawyer and dealing with adversaries day in and day out. Such courses can assist the lawyer in finding new approaches to problem solving, creative team building, the formation of win-win solutions, and can train lawyers help other lawyers and clients improve their leadership skills. Leadership development studies may very well be a good aspirin to a bad headache that too many lawyers face every day—chronic dissatisfaction with their professional lives as lawyers.

Poor reputation of lawyers within the society

The American Bar Association commissioned a study of lawyers in 2001[23] and the number one conclusion from that study was that "Lawyers have a poor reputation in American society. Americans say that lawyers are greedy, manipulative, and corrupt.

---

23 Robert Clifford, Chair, Litigation Section, "Opening Statement: Confronting our Critics," *Litigation* 28, no. 2 (winter 2001): American Bar Association.

Words like 'snakes' and 'sharks' were used by all of the groups in all of the markets tested." The report goes on to say:

> "Americans believe that the central place of lawyers in society enables them not only to manipulate the system but also to shape that very system."
>
> "Americans say that lawyers do a poor job of policing themselves. Bar associations are viewed not as protectors of the public but as clubs to protect lawyers."
>
> "Consumers are particularly frustrated with the fees lawyers charge for their services. They tell stories of lawyers who overcharge, are deceitful or coy about their fees, and won't account for the time they put on a case."
>
> "Consumers also tell stories of lawyers who drag out cases to buttress their fees, misrepresent their qualifications, and exacerbate conflict."

These indictments against lawyers and the legal profession are not often discussed in law school courses. Law students do not take courses of study to deal with the poor reputation of lawyers in society. Law students are initially unprepared to help reform and improve the reputation of the profession because they are not given the training or opportunity for leadership skills development necessary to lead the profession. The ABA report of 2001 stated, "Clearly, we must work to rebuild the public's trust in lawyering and to renew the respect society once held for its lawyers." Such an effort to rebuild the reputation was actually started in 1978 by the ABA itself. It failed. Although the 2001 ABA report concluded with the plea, "… we must first regain the respect and trust of the American people," no one to date has found any approach that appears to be succeeding at this all-important task.

This book makes the bold assertion that leadership development courses taught systematically to lawyers can help the profession significantly improve the reputation of lawyers in society at large. Today, just as in 1978, lawyers do not have the leadership training nor skills required to perform the leadership roles required of them. Second, lawyers today are not sufficiently concerned, as a whole, with fixing their poor reputation because they are more and more technically oriented professionals with few true leadership skills and aspirations. Leaders, by definition, care about and depend on their ability to develop and maintain excellent reputations. Leadership development courses for lawyers would assist lawyers in placing a greater emphasis on improving their reputation more than any current CLE course now available in the marketplace.

Lawyers are not taught in law school or CLE courses that reputation plays a key role in a profession's overall level of effectiveness. The ABA report acknowledges this point explicitly when it states:

> In short, the poor reputation of lawyers in society is not just a matter of professional pride. It directly impacts the relationship that lawyers have with their clients and can even impact the public's willingness to use lawyers to solve their problems. It impacts the public's belief in the way the justice system works.

Therefore, lawyers and the legal profession as a whole are unable, after thirty-seven years of concerted effort to turn the reputation of lawyers around at all. In fact, since 1978, the reputation of lawyers has, in all likelihood, actually declined.

The poor reputation of lawyers in the United States is not just a baseless prejudice against a powerful group of people. It is deeply rooted in negative experiences that people and organizations have with lawyers every day. Stan Sorrell, the former co-chairman of the board and CEO of the Calvert Group, Inc., an investment company that pioneered socially responsible investing used to refer to his legal department as the "sales prevention department." He disdained the multi-lawyer, multi-hour board meetings that cost thousands of dollars in legal fees and were often called by lawyers to deal with minor, technical points that could have been dealt with quickly and efficiently by anyone except lawyers.

Leadership development training programs are also designed to improve a key area where lawyers are notoriously bad, an area that hurts the reputation of lawyers every day. Lawyers have a reputation for being terrible listeners. Active listening skills taught in leadership development courses throughout the United States and abroad would be a very positive development in the legal education of lawyers. Substantial improvements in this skill and other leadership skills would, in all likelihood, pay off in significant dividends in improving the reputation of lawyers in the United States.

High departure rate for trained, qualified, and certified lawyers from the legal profession

In a recent article in *Forbes* magazine Helen Lavan stated, "The number of lawyers who are dissatisfied and will drop out of active practice is growing. Forbes magazine reports that in California the number of inactive attorneys has risen by 50% from a decade ago and in Massachusetts the number of inactive attorneys grew 3% in three years. Further, Lavan quotes a Forbes study that "a full 38% of attorneys say that they somewhat regret their career choice. Additionally, Harvard Law School counselors estimate that 20% to 30% of active attorneys are considering another career."[24]

Although no data could be located showing exactly how many lawyers who have graduated from law school and passed a bar exam are no longer practicing attorneys, all of our research indicates that this number is staggering and should be a major concern to every professional organization of lawyers and to individual lawyers themselves. Again, leadership development training could provide a useful approach to dealing with this problem of lawyers either leaving or wanting to leave the profession. First, leadership development training is designed to facilitate a person's search for the best fit between personal goals and values and the individual's professional choices. Successful leadership, as taught in leadership development courses, requires true commitment to accomplishing what needs to be accomplished in a person's job and work. This argues strongly for providing leadership development training to law students because it can help them create and find a path in the legal profession where they can love what they

24 Helen Lavan, "Dissatisfied Attorneys Have Plenty of Options," posted at CareerJournal.com.

do and find meaning in their profession. Clearly too many new lawyers do not like the choices they have made for early jobs in the profession.

Through the study of leadership theory, practice, skills, and aptitude, lawyers might well find new ways or structures through which to perform their work; new ways to organize their workloads, their firms, their client selection decisions, their cost structures and revenue needs, and their approaches to the adversary system; and new ways to do the work and accomplish the goals they want to accomplish and at the same time not feel compelled to abandon the profession for which they were trained. Leadership development courses directed by lawyers and former lawyers can result in courses that are tailored and based on a careful analysis as to why lawyers are so dissatisfied and are leaving the profession in great numbers. Such courses may well have the impact of helping stem the tide of lawyers who cannot wait to find their next line of work.

Growing economic pressures on law firms of all sizes, especially large firms

No leadership development course can change the laws of economics. The growing wave of mergers of law firms is the direct result of law firms requiring larger and larger revenues to cover the high fixed costs of providing high-end legal services to high-end clients. In addition, many clients want "one-stop shopping" in legal services today, because there is a general view among corporate clients that the fewer law firms the company employs on a regular basis, the better. Given that there are growing economic pressures on law firms of all sizes, how can leadership development courses address this growing concern in the legal profession?

Leadership development courses and instruction can address this challenge in part through the teamwork modules inherent in most sophisticated leadership courses today. Successful leadership practices can form the glue that helps merged law firms succeed and can help growing law firms integrate the ever-increasing number of lawyers and staff who work in these firms. Lawyers in large and small firms openly admit that their firms are silos with little interaction, and even less real cooperative work, among members of the firm in different sections or locales of the firm.

Private-sector companies have discovered the advantages of "matrix operations," in which people from different departments work as groups on projects and report to supervisors from many different departments, rather than working in silos and always reporting to someone from their own section or department. Law firms, however, generally have not had the leadership development education and skills training to implement these complex leadership and operational structures. Leadership development courses can help law firms struggling with the bottom line understand more about the benefits of innovation, business planning, strategic planning, and the implementation of novel leadership and decision-making approaches in the law firm environment. Leadership development courses can improve the ability of the people in the firm in mentoring junior associates and would allow and promote greater participation in decision-making in the law firm, thereby improving the decision-making ability of the organization as a whole.

The huge investment of companies in leadership development, the growing number of significant contracts signed by major law firms such as Reed Smith with the Wharton Business School, and DLA Piper Rudnick Gray Cary's recent leadership development training agreement signed with Harvard University suggest that leadership development courses can offer some significant help to the legal profession as it faces greater and greater economic pressures. In fact, the *Legal Week* article about DLA's contract with Harvard University stated that it was a "ground breaking move for the legal sector."

High levels of client dissatisfaction and formal complaints (including ethical complaints) and malpractice actions against lawyers

Although this item is related to the poor reputation that lawyers have earned over the past fifty years, it is different from the reputation problem in terms of how leadership development courses could provide some form of solution. As stated earlier, lawyers are often viewed as being poor listeners, and the lack of listening skills get lawyers in trouble with clients. Lawyers also often fail to communicate on a regular basis with clients, fail to return phone calls promptly, fail to keep clients up-to-date on their matters, fail to consult with clients on important matters of tactics and strategies, and even often fail to listen well enough to understand the client's real goals and objectives. Leadership training, especially the concepts inherent in the area of servant leadership made popular by Robert Greenleaf (described along with the many other brands of leadership in Appendix A), provides crucial tools, skills, and practices that can squarely address the problems associated with poor client communication and high levels of client dissatisfaction.

Leadership development training, especially the leadership behavioral assessments that are often a component of these programs, can alert lawyers and law firms to areas where lawyers and staffs in firms and legal organizations may have blind spots regarding their ability to work successfully with clients and leading legal organizations. Very rarely are lawyers sued by clients or admonished by bar associations for not knowing the technical aspects of the law. Rather, it is more often poor client relationship skills that subject them and their clients to a less-than-perfect relationship and a bad result for the client.

Leadership development training courses can assist lawyers and legal administrators with seeing the warning signs in a law firm or in a client relationship that reveal that things are not going well in the firm or with the client early enough to take successful actions to avoid larger problems down the road. Leadership development courses will assist lawyers in better understanding their client's true goals and in meeting them or parting ways with a client at a stage that is early enough in the relationship not to cause harm to either the lawyer or the client. Leadership development courses teach responsiveness and service in such a manner that for lawyers who take these courses, it will be less likely that a lawyer would not return fifty-two separate phone calls and letters from a client (a true story known to this author). That lawyer appropriately faced a bar association tribunal for her failure to communicate with a client. A leadership development course could have made a huge difference to the lawyer and the client in this instance and in many similar instances.

Many leadership development courses today have an ethics component deeply ingrained in the course. Although there is no unified theory of ethical leadership, much work is being done at the academic level by Joann Ciulla, Ph.D., of the University of Richmond's Jepson School of Leadership and others to improve the integration of ethics into the teaching and theoretical framework of leadership development. The ethics components of leadership development training are quite different from the ethics training of lawyers in traditional CLE courses. Traditionally, lawyers learn "situational ethics" based on the canons of ethics approved by each bar association and the Model Rules of Professional Conduct promulgated by the Center for Professional Responsibility of the American Bar Association. These ethical courses focus on such issues as conflicts of interest, defining the scope of the lawyer-client relationship; safekeeping and managing a client's property; informing a client of all key issues, facts, and occurrences related to their matters; duties to disclose or not disclose client-provided information; duties to former clients; candor toward a tribunal; dealing with unrepresented persons; and advertising, among other topics. Leadership development courses for lawyers and legal staff designed by lawyers, such as the one created by Sam Cassidy, Esquire, chair of the Department of Business Ethics and Legal Studies at the Daniels College of Business, University of Denver, includes such topics as

- Challenging the value of competition—X, Y game in legal practice
- Decision-making frameworks for leaders with exercises
- How do we make decisions when values are in conflict?
- Considering the consequences of decisions
- Duties owed to stakeholders
- Exercises in decisionmaking
- Virtues of professionals—Kohlberg's theory of moral development

The substantial number of ethical complaints that the legal profession must process and decide each year causes great concern among those who ponder seriously the future of the legal profession. These ethical complaints cost clients and the legal profession millions of dollars as well. Alternative approaches to teaching ethics, as provided by the leadership development literature and courses on leadership that have a strong ethical perspective may well prove to be a very strong complement to the ethical training lawyers receive today.

Growing levels of associate turnover

Although this item is related to the issue regarding the large number of lawyers leaving the practice of law, from a leadership development perspective, it is quite different. Associates leave law firms for many reasons, and often the law firm management wants them to leave because they are not succeeding in the firm or are not going to make partner. Leadership development programs can help provide an environment where associates are given mentors in the firm who have been trained through leadership development courses to know how to be a successful leader, and teach others to be successful leaders. Research in the human resource literature shows that one of the most common reasons why people leave their companies is they believe the quality of their manager or management in general at the company is poor.

If lawyers at firms learned how to provide mentoring to associates and law firms provided better leadership training to associates, we anticipate that communication would flow much better between associates and other, more senior lawyers in the firm. We believe that if communication flowed more evenly in the firm and mentoring activities were improved, associates would be less interested in finding another firm or leaving the profession. Leadership development training can become a competitive advantage for law firms because it can reduce lawyer turnover and improve retention rates of those associates the firm wants to retain. In addition, leadership development courses will likely result in the law firm finding new ways to include associates in some of the governance practices of the firm. This will also help address associate retention challenges that law firms have.

Prevalence of outdated governance practices at law firms

It is beyond the scope of this book to provide a laundry list of outmoded governance practices that exist in many law firms today. Many law firms have one or two people who make all key business decisions and many of the professional legal decisions in the firm. Other firms may use a small management committee comprised of only one to three lawyers to make all compensation decisions for the firm. Many firms encourage the creation of silos by giving lawyers completely free reign in their business development practices and in how they provide legal services. These management practices often result in a law firm providing a widely varying quality of legal services and even fee arrangements depending on which lawyer in the firm a client hires.

Leadership development programs can assist senior managers in law firms and legal organizations in developing more inclusive approaches to decision-making, creating new ways to organize a firm's business development practices, and in improving compensation decisions to meet the dual tests of rewarding business generation and rewarding professional excellence. Leadership development programs, if administered properly, can guide a law firm or legal organization toward developing innovative management approaches. If senior management of law firms that use old-style, top-down management structures are assisted in developing more participatory management programs, the recruiting and retention of top level associates and new partners will become easier because these associates and partners will know from the first day on the job, and even before, that their ideas regarding how the firm should be run will be taken into account by senior management.

The concept of "leader of leaders" is quite apt for the role of senior management of law firms today. Senior partners and law firm administrators of large law firms must be able to "steer the ship," but one cannot steer complex ships today without receiving excellent feedback from many different stations or persons on the ship. One can not steer complex ships either if one is a micromanager, trying to supervise and instruct each person working on the ship regarding each task the person has to perform. Micromanagement may have been a viable leadership approach in simpler times. However, micromanagement is no longer an appropriate leadership style for the top echelons of management in today's complex legal organizations. Leadership development courses and training sessions can help show senior management of law firms how to refine and adapt their leadership skills. Such courses can show younger associates and new partners how to contribute in a positive manner to the improvement of the firm.

Continuing evidence of a glass ceiling for women in law firms

Although the chapter on women and leadership addressed this issue in detail, there are two additional areas where leadership development programs could have a huge impact on helping women succeed to partnership or leadership positions in law firms, legal organizations, in corporate legal staffs, and in government agencies. First, such programs could give women the leadership skills and training they need to deal more successfully with the male leadership of most legal organizations. Second, leadership development programs could provide men in legal organizations with a new appreciation of the special challenges that women face in legal-oriented environments. This new understanding could lead men who currently have the decision-making power in these organizations to understand more fully and better appreciate the value of sharing power with women in the firm at earlier stages in their careers than in the past. The legal profession is headed toward great difficulty if it cannot better integrate women into the leadership positions of its profession.

The loss of women lawyers who are leaving the profession is a serious blow to the profession and to the women who feel forced out of the profession. It is a loss to clients who have developed a successful and trusting relationship with them and other potential clients who could benefit from their services. It is a loss to the firms who could benefit from their expertise. Leadership development courses and training could contribute to the profession more successfully addressing many of the challenges that women face in the legal profession in rising to the top of firms, corporate legal staffs, and in government agencies.

Client challenges to paying increasingly large legal bills and insistence on alternative billing structures

Leadership development and entrepreneurship are decidedly different subjects that require different teaching platforms. As an adjunct professor who has taught courses in both subject areas, entrepreneurship and leadership development, I have found that there is much overlap in these two disciplines. Leadership development courses can assist participants in looking at the status quo as only one alternative to how the future might be. Leadership development courses are designed to open up the mind to pursuing and embracing innovation. Such innovations in the creation of alternative billing structures may well be needed as the billable hour becomes more and more the subject of client dissatisfaction and outright attack. Leadership development courses could also provide attorneys better insight and practical tools in communicating with their clients at every stage of representation their best estimates of the costs and benefits of each element of the representation.

Providing legal services is expensive, and no leadership development course can change this. However, leadership development courses can assist lawyers in becoming better communicators with clients to show them why the expected cost of the representation is so high and can give lawyers a stronger willingness to master alternative billing structures that may provide a win-win solution for both the lawyer and the client.

Increasing competition and growing use of questionable means to obtain clients/business

There are many new marketing and business development courses for lawyers on the market today. There is a new professional position called "marketing director" in law firms. There is a growing trend for advertising for lawyers and law firms throughout the United States. The old-fashioned way lawyers obtained business was by demonstrating their leadership and legal skills in client matters, in community organizations, through writing insightful articles that showed technical and analytical mastery over

THE VALUE OF LEADERSHIP DEVELOPMENT IN THE PROFESSION

an area of law and by giving speeches throughout the community related to their civic and nonprofit volunteer efforts. Now, a thirty-second advertisement puts a lawyer or law firm in front of millions of viewers who apparently hire the advertising lawyer often enough to justify the advertising expense.

There will always be lawyer advertising. However, leadership development courses that promote the lawyer's ability to achieve great results for clients, that improve the lawyer's ability to achieve success in providing community and civic leadership, that promote the lawyer's giving speeches and writing articles, and that in general help place the lawyer in a favorable light in the community, may well prove to be a much more cost-effective tool in marketing services and business development for the lawyer than high-priced advertising. In spite of large-scale advertising, client development in the legal profession will always continue to be very relationship oriented, including word-of-mouth marketing we call referrals. Frequently, lawyers refer clients to other lawyers, without even asking for a referral fee. They do this often based on the reputation of the lawyer to whom they refer business and the exacting needs of a particular client for a specialist. Trust is still a very important component of the referral process among lawyers.

Leadership development courses, as explained previously, give lawyers and law firms a strategic advantage in obtaining and excelling in leadership activities in the community that can put lawyers and their reputations in a very favorable light with potential clients, with the media, and with other lawyers. In addition to making the lawyer better known in the community in a favorable way, leadership development courses could allow a lawyer to upgrade his or her client base, and to be hired as this author has been on numerous occasions for the lawyer's leadership skills rather than merely for specialized legal expertise. In this era of increasing specialization among lawyers, enhancing the skill mix and reputation of lawyers and law firms as a direct result of leadership development courses may well be an excellent, cost-effective business development strategy.

Increasing lack of civility among lawyers

Entire books like *The Betrayed Profession: Lawyering at the end of the Twentieth Century* by Sol M. Linowitz and Martin Mayer, have been devoted to the increasing lack of civility among lawyers.[25] Even in Nova Scotia the Barrister's Society has recently appointed a Task Force on Professional Civility. The Supreme Court of Illinois in 2001 created a committee on professionalism designed to address the growing problem of lack of civility among lawyers in that state.

There are many reasons for this disturbing trend in the profession. The growth and "nationalization" of the legal profession means that there is less likelihood that one particular lawyer will have a case against another particular lawyer on a repeated basis. Having many cases with a known counsel on the other side used to promote civility because lawyers developed professional relationships so that they could work day in and day out with the lawyers they opposed on a regular basis. Today, two lawyers may square off against each other only once, and for a short period of time, at that. The result is that part of the social fabric of the legal community has been shredded, and lawyers are much more aggressive in being hostile, rude, and even taking advantage of another lawyer, believing it will not come back to haunt them in the future.

Although leadership development courses cannot be the complete answer to improving civility in the legal profession, the perspective of "respect for all parties" inherent in many leadership development courses would go far toward helping lawyers understand how being civil to other lawyers can benefit them, their clients, the reputation of lawyers, and the legal profession as a whole. Often lawyers will say they are not civil to other attorneys because the other attorneys are not civil to them. This is precisely where leadership development teaching can play a huge role. The lawyers who say that they are not civil to other attorneys because the other attorneys are not civil to them are clearly acting as *followers* and letting the other attorney manage the tenor of the discourse, relationship, and conversation. Recently I sat in the trial of several defendants charged in the theft of millions of dollars from

---

25 Sol M. Linowitz and Martin Mayer, *The Betrayed Profession: Lawyering at the End of the Twentieth Century*, Johns Hopkins University Press (Baltimore, MD 2000).

the Washington Teachers Union in Washington, D.C. After one attorney sent a broad subpoena to one of the defendants' counsel during trial, and after the judge instructed the lawyers to try and work out their discovery dispute, the lawyer for the defendant, in the courtroom just after court recessed, verbally attacked the other counsel for sending the subpoena in the first place and was anything but civil to the other counsel.

Leadership development courses instruct participants in how to manage conversations. These courses go to great lengths to teach participants how to at least manage the participants' part of the conversation according to their standards, and not the standards of others. The teaching of communication standards is subtle, but important. For these reasons, leadership development courses would, in all likelihood, be of great benefit to the legal profession in improving civility among lawyers.

Increasing delays in litigation, arbitrations, and even mediations

The litigation explosion of the last forty years has created a huge backlog in our courts. Lawyers often find it in their client's interest to seek delay to avoid the day of reckoning. As Frank Flegal, the late, great civil procedure professor at Georgetown University's Law Center stated at the end of the first-year civil procedure course, "I have now taught you how to handle a case in the courts properly. You can also use these procedures to delay matters for years. Do not use what I have taught you to do this." This simple statement is consistent with the basic teaching of leadership development courses.

Statements like "Justice delayed is justice denied" and "A denial of justice anywhere is a threat to justice everywhere" (Dr. Martin Luther King) are central tenants of leadership development books and courses. Leadership development courses teach people to look at the big picture, and although they would not teach anyone to sacrifice a client's legitimate interests in a matter to achieve a quick resolution of matter, they teach people not to create unnecessary delay or take advantage of situations just for the short-term gain of one person at the direct expense of another person.

The embedded concepts of seeking win-win solutions, of using the rules for their intended purpose and not just for delaying justice, and of making recommendations to clients that represent fair treatment to all even when the client does not want to hear such a recommendation, represent the hallmark of leadership development education as currently taught in the United States. Such teachings could have a significant impact on the enormous backlog of client matters awaiting their day in court.

High levels of substance abuse among lawyers, affecting their ability to serve clients' needs

A final area where leadership development courses can play an important role in helping the legal profession deal with a serious problem is in the area of substance abuse. Due to the potential positive impacts discussed above, it is reasonable to believe that large-scale leadership development training can reduce some of the causes related to substance abuse among lawyers. In addition, leadership development courses are designed to assist people in taking action in supporting others to deal directly with the problems they face. Too often, lawyers know of other lawyers who have substance-related challenges, yet do nothing and say nothing. Leadership development courses often propel individuals to take responsibility at a new level towards others and could result in lawyers directly approaching others they suspect or know have substance- or alcohol-related problems. Back in 1988 Michael A. Bloom documented the high incidence of alcoholism among lawyers.[26] The American Bar Association has even produced a videotape, *Alcoholism and the Intervention Process*, focusing on a (fictional) alcohol-dependent Judge. Many other articles and other videotapes address this serious problem.

No leadership development course alone can prevent or cure an alcohol or substance addiction. However, when a lawyer is alcohol or substance "impaired," clients often suffer, and the legal profession as part of its self-policing function has a duty to take significant steps to protect the public from those lawyers who begin to fail their clients because of these problems. The legal profession has made little documented progress in this area over the

---
26 Michael A. Bloom, "Lawyers and Alcoholism: Is It Time for a New Approach?" *Temple Law Review* 61 (1988): 1409.

past thirty years. Leadership development courses could be one of the catalysts for addressing the problem more successfully than has been done in the past.

These suggested examples of how leadership development courses can begin to address some of the major challenges of the legal profession admittedly are at this stage be based on reason, logic, and inference, because lawyers have not taken leadership developments courses in any great number before the publishing of this book. However, knowing the problems of the legal profession firsthand, being a lawyer for over twenty-three years, and being familiar with the teachings of the leadership development courses and the leadership development literature, all point to same conclusion: the body of knowledge, skills, theories, and practices of leadership development courses could yield substantial benefits to the legal profession.

This book has one goal: the start of a new era of the legal profession and lawyers taking seriously the teachings of the leadership development field and its advances over the past forty years. The final chapter of this book discusses how the future of the legal profession will likely begin to embrace the leadership development field and take its findings, research, approaches, testing instruments, workbooks, exercises, and courses more seriously in the very near future.

CHAPTER EIGHT
THE FUTURE OF LEADERSHIP EDUCATION IN THE LEGAL PROFESSION

With law firms such as Reed Smith and DLA Piper Rudnick Gray Carey already signing large-scale contracts for leadership development training with Wharton and Harvard, some would say the future is already here. With Holmes, Roberts and Owens becoming the first law firm in the western United States considering investing in leadership coaching for its lawyers, and with Colorado becoming one of the first states to approve a CLE course that teaches leadership for lawyers that is open to all lawyers in the United States, one could argue that the future of leadership education for lawyers is already spreading throughout the United States.

When this book was conceived in 2001, none of these things had happened. Even in 2004, when I gave the speech "Leadership Education for Lawyers: Potential and Challenges" to the Association of Continuing Legal Educators' Annual Convention, the number of skeptics in the audience far outweighed those who wanted their bar associations immediately to begin to offer or even approve leadership development courses for continuing legal education credit. (This speech is included in Appendix B of this book).

Chapter 5 showed that a strong business case can be made for leadership development courses for the legal profession. Bar associations and state supreme courts have the ultimate power to accelerate the creation and delivery of leadership development courses for lawyers because they are instrumental in approving such courses for CLE credit. Today, we have CLE-approved courses in time management, PowerPoint, and other areas of education far more removed from basic lawyering and client service than leadership development. It is time for a change.

Law firms will begin to purchase large-scale leadership development training for their lawyers when they realize that these educational and training efforts will not only improve the quality of legal services they provide to their clients, but also will improve the quality of the professional experiences of their lawyers and staff and ultimately will improve the bottom line of the law firms. Leadership development courses represent a strong, innovative way to improve the reputation of lawyers, address the growing lack of civility, and address some of the major ills affecting our profession.

Of course, lawyers have always been free to enroll in leadership development courses in the past and have by and large chosen not to do so. As Tony Grundy, my coauthor in *Breakthrough, Inc.: High Growth Strategies for Entrepreneurial Organizations*, cogently explained, much of the behavior in an industry can be explained by understanding the "industry mind-set."[27] The industry mind-set of the legal profession has been that leadership development courses are not needed by lawyers. This book and the challenges faced by the legal profession, plus the advances over the past several decades in the leadership development literature, in leadership assessment tools, and leadership development courses, all combine to make leadership development courses very useful to the lawyer of today and especially the lawyer of the future.

CONCLUSION

Evolution by its nature has a sense of inevitability. The practice of leadership through an elitist-oriented, top-down approach that is reserved for the few has been embraced by many professionals in the legal profession. This book makes the bold claim that the predominant leadership style in the legal profession will evolve over time to a more participatory leadership approach. The current leaders of law firms and other legal organizations who reserve all power to themselves will not willingly give up their positions of authority. But winning comes to those who recognize the next wave of change and get ahead of the curve. When cutting-edge law firms and legal organizations begin to emphasize participatory leadership, distribute leadership tasks more broadly

---

27 Herb Rubenstein and Tony Grundy, *Breakthrough, Inc.: High Growth Strategies for Entrepreneurial Organizations* (Prentice Hall/Financial Times, 1999).

throughout their organizations, and begin to succeed and gain a recognizable competitive advantage, cultures will begin to rapidly change in other law firms and legal organizations. Over time, the majority of people in the legal profession will begin to support the idea that when leadership development is taught more broadly to lawyers and others in the legal profession, this will result in better law firms, legal organizations, and workplace environments. Leadership development education for people in the legal profession can enhance performance, improve retention levels, provide better financial results, and help to create healthier work environments. As these breakthroughs begin to occur, we expect leaders in the legal profession will vote with their pocketbooks to invest in leadership development programs for lawyers and staff who work in the legal profession.

As law firms and legal organizations empower, encourage, and allow their employees, clients, vendors, and even adversaries step up as leaders, the result will be that leadership development training will be implemented quite quickly throughout the profession. Human capital, an individual's ability and competence to think, act, direct, understand, and lead, has evolved too far to expect employees in the legal profession to give their best when they are not allowed to lead and are forced to utilize only a small percentage of their skills, knowledge, and abilities in the key decision-making processes where they work. Law firms and legal organizations will achieve the next burst in human and organizational productivity by tapping into their employees' full ability to contribute to the organization. Law firms and legal organizations will dramatically improve by delegating leadership tasks and responsibilities to such an extent to allow all employees the opportunity to deploy all of their talents and knowledge all of the time. This can occur only when significant leadership development programs are offered to and are taken by people in the legal profession.

As Larry Downs suggested, improved management skills and leadership skills will be the next "killer app" in the legal profession.[28] We have seen this evolution in leadership development courses already start in the worlds of business, education, psychology, engineering, and other professions. We see it in the flat organizations that constitute many of the innovative, productive

---

28 Larry Downs, "The Killer App," *Harvard Business Review* (December 2004): Cambridge, MD.

high-tech and knowledge industry workplaces in the U.S. and throughout the world today.

The challenge facing the legal profession today is to make this movement from leadership by the few to leadership by the many pervasive and well supported in law firms and legal organizations. This book and the outlines for the leadership courses set forth in this book are a small step toward dealing with the admonition of Gabriella de Audrey, a great artist, musician, and co-founder of the Maryland State Opera Society, who said,

"Don't put talent where it can't get out."

That should be an important goal of law firm administrators, law firm chairmen, judges, heads of legal organizations, general counsels, attorneys general, sole practitioners, and educators in the field of law. A new day is dawning in which a lawyer trained in leadership development will be a better lawyer than one not trained in leadership development. Firms and organizations that train their employees in the art of leadership development will have a decided advantage over those firms and organizations that stand by the old model of "senior partner knows best." We see the future in the Reed Smith and DLA Piper Rudnick Gray Carey contracts for leadership development. We see the future in the continuing legal education credits that are finally starting to be awarded for leadership development courses and training.

Today, the legal profession needs significant breakthroughs in order to

- improve its productivity,
- improve its reputation,
- improve its civility,
- improve its ability to serve clients at a reasonable cost,
- improve its employee retention and satisfaction,
- improve its ability to reduce burnout,
- reduce substance abuse among lawyers, and
- help lawyers cope with the stress.

THE FUTURE OF LEADERSHIP EDUCATION IN THE PROFESSION

Leadership development education and training is not the panacea that will solve every challenge of the legal profession. However, it is the basic premise of this book that leadership development education and training could be a major step in the right direction to improving the legal profession for our practitioners, our clients, and the society at large which we proudly serve.

APPENDIX A

NINETY BRANDS OF LEADERSHIP DEFINED AND EXPLAINED

We define approximately ninety brands of leadership currently that are on the market. We have divided them into the following sixteen categories.

1. Ethical Leadership
2. Bad/Dysfunctional Leadership
3. Single-Leader Focus
4. Interactive Focus
5. Follower Focus
6. Multileader Focus
7. New Challenge Orientation
8. Nontraditional Organization
9. Results Orientation
10. Leadership Development/Training
11. Situational Leadership
12. Team Orientation Leadership
13. Traditional Leadership Brands
14. Visionary Leadership
15. Holistic Follower Orientation
16. Holistic Leader Orientation

We believe these categories accurately describe and categorize the types of leadership brands being taught today.

Category 1
Ethical Leadership

Character-based leadership: Character-based leaders place the common good at the core of their goals, and their leadership demonstrates concern for the personal development of their followers. Successful character-based leadership improves productivity and decreases worker turnover, because followers sense that they are assets and not expenses. In turn, this improves customer service and the quality of products overall. This leadership style or brand combines principle-centered leadership and servant leadership in a way that combines principle-centered leadership's integrity with the servant leadership's foundational goal of helping others.

Conscious leadership: John Renesch, author of numerous books on business, coined the term "conscious leadership" to describe leadership that originates from an individual's inner moral sense. According to Renesch, the conscious leader intuitively knows right from wrong and leads from a moral compass instead of from a prescribed code. Such leaders are likely to spontaneously take the lead when they sense a leadership vacuum, regardless of their official position. Conscious leadership radiates outward from the individual and seeks to take into account the group consciousness of all people involved in a project.

Contributory leadership: This term denotes leaders whose purpose and actions are designed almost exclusively to contribute to an improvement of an organization, the members of the organization, and the society at large. Contributory leadership promotes the sharing of leadership tasks and decisions quite broadly.

Ethical leadership: This brand of leadership, through the work of Jo Ann Ciulla, Ph.D., professor of leadership at the Jepson School of Leadership of the University of Richmond, and others may someday develop into a full-blown theory of leadership. Ethical leadership is leadership that is guided by and accepts ethical constraints and does not accept the theory that the goal of leadership is to accomplish a result regardless of the means used to achieve the desired result.

Inspired leadership: This brand of leadership focuses on individually based, ethical leadership. Jamie Walters of Ivy Sea claims, "This very notion of inspired leadership obviously carries with it a self-referencing connection to ethics, integrity, compassion, dignity, and other 'heart-centered' and Spirit-derived reference points."

Servant leadership: The term "servant leader" was coined by Robert Greenleaf in his book, *Servant Leadership*. He describes servant leaders as those who begin with the desire to serve and then gradually develop the aspiration to lead others. Greenleaf contrasts servant leadership with his understanding that some people want to lead first, and only serve others as an ancillary objective. Thus, a spectrum exists where servant leaders and narcissistic leaders are two extremes. Ultimately, the difference in these two brands or types of leaders is whether the leader is more concerned with personal recognition and ego or with the personal growth and well-being of his or her followers and the community the leader serves. Servant leaders are inclusive, and want to serve their community and use their leadership skills and position to expand the leadership roles and capacities of those they serve. Often servant leaders do not hold formal leadership position but lead with influence and encourage collaboration among their followers. Servant leaders emphasize and demonstrate how ethics is an integral part of leadership through the example they set for others.

Steward leadership: Peter Block and Katherine Tyler Scott, President, Trustee Leadership Development, have written several influential books on this brand of leadership. This brand of leadership says that leaders are responsible for making decisions about and managing the resources over which the leader has control or influence. Steward leaders manage these resources ethically and solely in the interest of the people whose resource the leader is designated to manage. In the corporate world, steward leadership includes being a good leader of people, a good steward of products and services, and a leader of the community. It maintains that the power to lead originates from below and is exclusively for the benefit of others. This type of leadership also has strong religious connotations and specifically rejects exploiting power and leadership opportunities for the benefit of the leader.

Trustee leadership: This brand of leadership popularized by Katherine Tyler Scott and others is directed to boards of directors and describes how leaders balance the relationship between their self-interest and the good of their followers and community. Trustee leaders believe that their role as leaders is completely tied to the common good, and they try to integrate the personal aspects of being a leader with professional, individual, and community interests that grow out of their leadership actions. Trustee leadership can apply in the for-profit, nonprofit, political, and policy realms. James Kouzes, author of *The Leadership Challenges*, writes that "you cannot lead others until you have first led yourself through a struggle of opposing values." Trustee leaders both develop a vision and participate as trustees of the leadership position and status that others have conferred upon them.

Values-based leadership: This brand of leadership requires the leader to understand the different and sometimes contrasting ideas, values, and needs of those involved in a project or organization and, then articulate the moral and ethical values and principles upon which the leader bases his or her decisions and actions. People from Steve Jobs, the cofounder of Apple Computer, Inc. to General Norman Schwartzkopf claim that values based leadership is most important in today's business world and in public life because people who care about similar values work best together and can build the bonds of trust required for successful leadership. Values-based leadership encourages trust and can be very helpful when building interpersonal relationships. Values-based leadership includes three key areas, effectiveness, morality, and a focus on long-term goals.

Values-centered leadership: William J. O'Brien has written extensively about this leadership approach in his book, *The Soul of Corporate Leadership: Guidelines for Value-Centered Governance*. This brand of leadership occurs when the values of the leader and the values of the followers are fused and become one, emanating from either direction. In such an atmosphere, followers are involved and motivated to help others and to be a part of something larger than themselves. Sam Walton, founder of Wal-Mart, mastered this leadership technique. The Wal-Mart training program teaches each trainee the personal values of the founder and subsequently the values of the corporation. Each follower is then expected to embrace these values, not only at work, but also in his or her personal life. Ideally, this type of leadership creates an environment where followers promote, demonstrate, and defend the organization's values.

Category 2
Bad/Dysfunctional Leadership

Bogus leadership: This is opposite of conscious leadership. Bogus leadership is leadership occurs when leaders follow a narrow or scripted type of leadership that does not reflect who they are. Their insistence on following a single leadership paradigm limits their thinking, giving them fewer options and causing them to act more slowly than conscious leaders, who lead from their moral compass and group consciousness.

Narcissistic leadership: This type of leadership occurs when leaders are motivated primarily by their desire to serve their egos. Generally, narcissistic leaders keep very high profiles. It should be clear that narcissistic leadership does not necessarily mean unproductive leadership. Michael Maccoby, author of *The Productive Narcissist: The Promise and Peril of Visionary Leaders*, argues that narcissistic leaders are generally useful in times of transition or turbulence because they have the personal popularity and charisma to make massive changes. Over time, however, these leaders tend to become unrealistic dreamers, and their leadership styles can drag down their companies. Narcissistic leaders tend to ignore advice and take a top-down approach to leading. Narcissistic leaders are marked by great vision and many followers, who are often more personally loyal to the narcissistic leader than to his or her vision and policies. The weaknesses of narcissistic leaders include over-sensitivity to criticism, lack of empathy, poor listening skills, distaste for mentoring, and an excessive desire to compete.

Reactive leadership: This leadership style or brand is the opposite of proactive leadership. Reactive leaders expect and assume the worst from their followers, sometimes treating them as if they were children. Reactive leaders tend to focus on weaknesses and negatives, rarely providing positive encouragement. Reactive leaders address issues only after they occur, instead of anticipating and handling future challenges. This creates an air of crisis, making the leader seem disorganized. To further complicate matters, reactive leaders are often unclear about their goals and lack a vision for the future. Because of these attributes, reactive leaders tend to punish employees after the fact rather than guide them toward a clear goal in advance.

Toxic leadership: This leadership style is also called "destructive leadership." It has been studied by Jean Lipman-Blumen in her book, *The Allure of Toxic Leaders: Why We Follow Destructive Bosses.* This brand of leadership harms an organization by focusing relentlessly on short-term goals. Toxic leadership ignores the morale of followers and their working conditions. Ultimately, toxic leaders can be identified by the long-term effects of their destructive behavior. Their followers perform poorly for several reasons. First, they often feel compelled to overfocus on the short run. Second, they are discouraged by the myopic focus on the bottom line and the poor choices inherent in their leadership style. Third, toxic leaders have poor interpersonal skills, which hurt the self-esteem of their followers, adversely affecting the entire working environment. Fourth, toxic leaders value being in control, and they will often go to great lengths in order to preserve their leadership position.

Category 3
Single Leader Focus

Alpha male leadership: This brand of leadership, discussed at length by Arnold M. Ludwig in his book, *King of the Mountain*, suggests that human beings, like apes and wolves, are hardwired and instinctively driven to have a dominant male be a leader of a social group. Often this leadership brand assigns great weight to physical characteristics as leading predictors of who will emerge as the leader and dominant person in the group. This brand of leadership is gender oriented in a way that is rejected by many people today. But Ludwig suggests that this brand of leadership is

NINETY BRANDS OF LEADERSHIP DEFINED AND EXPLAINED

displayed in many of the 1,941 heads of nations during the twentieth century.

Assigned leadership: This brand refers to leadership based on positions or titles. It is similar to hereditary leadership except that, instead of attaining a leadership position through death (usually of a father), an assigned leader is appointed based on heredity, merit, or other factors. It is very popular in the military. In some cases, assigned leaders are insecure in their positions because they have no popular base. This insecurity often manifests itself as authoritarian, and sometimes even dictatorial, leadership. Accountability is often important to counteract some of the potential negative behavior associated with this type of leadership.

Authentic leadership: This brand advocated by Kevin Cashman, author of *Leadership from the Inside Out,* defines authentic leadership as the leadership that radiates from the core of a person. He states, "leadership is authentic self-expression that creates value." Cashman defines five key areas of authentic leadership. (1) Knowing oneself authentically. (2) Listening authentically. (3) Expressing one's self authentically. (4) Appreciating authentically. (5) Serving authentically. In order to be an authentic leader, a person must serve first and lead second. Authentic leaders seek to set an example for all of their followers and for other leaders through their actions and how they approach their leadership responsibilities.

Leadership by example: This brand is adopted by leaders who seek to use their own actions as a guide to their followers. In short, leadership by example implies that leaders should do everything with the same ethical and quality standards that they require of others. There are two parts to this type of leadership: (1) doing what should be done in every situation and (2) doing it according to high standards of exemplary behavior. Leadership by example can have the positive effect of inspiring followers to have the same goals and commitment as leaders and to adopt their methods and approaches to leadership tasks.

Charismatic leadership: This brand of leadership, discussed in the 1800s by Max Weber and many others, is distinguished from other types of leadership because charismatic leaders inspire people to follow them. Charismatic leaders impress their own visions and goals upon their followers and make their followers see things the way they do. Charismatic leaders radiate self-confidence, fearlessly lead, and know how to communicate their positions and ideas without embarrassment or reservation. Followers often turn to charismatic leaders during times of organizational, corporate, or social turmoil. Charismatic leadership tends to follow the traditional or heroic leadership model. Charismatic leaders lead from the top down and followers generally do not participate in the decision-making process. One great danger of this brand of leadership is that followers can become blind to what the leader is actually doing and never question the results the leader is actually trying to achieve.

Directive leadership: This brand of leadership is the opposite of participative leadership. In times of crisis, people tend to turn to directive leaders, because directive leadership points the way to safety. Directive leaders take charge, make decisions, and expect their decisions to be implemented without question. They are willing to revise goals and provide solutions unilaterally, using the traditional top-down approaches to leading. When the difficult times are past, followers often prefer leaders who are less directive, instead favoring those who seek input before making decisions. Modern history provides numerous examples of directive leadership. For example, democracies tend to reelect directive leaders during times of war. Wartime presidents tend to be more decisive and unilateral than others, and people accept and welcome these traits in times of war or crisis. When the crisis passes, however, the heavy-handed, dictatorial methods of some directive leaders often become unpopular with the voting public. This type of leadership is often replaced by a leader who is more participatory, collaborative, and consultative.

Integrated leadership: This brand of leadership was popularized by Ken Rafferty of Executive Consulting, who argues that integrated leadership involves all aspects of the human condition and creates new ways to get people involved in what they are doing, He says that integrated leadership helps executives understand the power and usefulness of embracing values, trust, participation, learning, creating, and sharing within the work environment. It also involves connecting the various people and departments in an organization with one another to achieve a common purpose decided upon by an organization through involving all of the members of the organization in setting the tone and direction for the organization.

Leaders building leaders: This brand or model of leadership has been promoted by Peter Drucker, Jack Welch, and many others. The basic tenet of this brand of leadership is that the primary purpose of a leader is to build up the capabilities of followers so that one can step in and take over should a leader, for any reason, not be able or willing to lead further. The key is that in order for a company to maintain success, the current leaders must continually prepare future leaders. Leaders building leaders is a results-based leadership strategy that promotes future leaders by encouraging "upward" or "trickle-up" leadership and by using 360-degree feedback and other leadership assessment tools. The leaders building leaders brand helps organizations increase their leadership resources, eases transitions, and increases stability.

Leadership at every step: This brand of leadership suggests that leadership is a full-time, 24/7 job and is a lifelong process instead of something that one can do on occasion or as an isolated act during a lifetime. It is an approach used by organizations that believe that leadership can and should occur in every part of an organization and at all times. Leadership at every step implies that all people can lead and have a responsibility to do so.

Postmortem leadership: This brand of leadership describes the influence strong, heroic leaders can have on their successors and organizations after they leave. This type of leadership can have a profound impact on policy and decision making in the future of many organizations. Postmortem leadership occurs when current leaders try to govern using the formulas and ideas of their predecessor(s) instead of creating their own or following the desires of their followers as they evolve.

Supportive leadership: In *Art of Supportive Leadership*, J. Donald Walters argues a supportive leader always recognizes that people are very important and not just tools for the leaders to use. Supportive leaders are loyal to and supportive of their followers. The classic example of this type of leadership is the general who stays at the front with his troops, despite the dangers to himself. Supportive leaders emphasize having high levels of confidence in and improving the competence in their followers. Supportive leaders are not micromanagers and give their followers substantial room to contribute to leadership decisions and to exhibit leadership behaviors.

Versatile leadership: Robert Kaiser and Robert Kaplan state that versatile leadership consists of a synthesis between balanced leadership and strategic leadership. The versatile leader must balance of leadership traits and approaches at each moment. This type of leadership is dynamic and situationally determined.

Category 4
Interactive Focus

Achievement-oriented leadership: This brand of leadership is one aspect of Robert House's path-goal theory discussed in the text of this book. This type of leader sets high goals and difficult challenges for both the leader and the team. This type of leader also provides encouragement for the members and expresses confidence in the ability of the group to complete the assigned task. Achievement-oriented leaders are ultimately interested results, but their leadership focuses on more than just the bottom line. By motivating followers, by challenging them, and by giving positive feedback, this leader can promote improved productivity.

Appreciative leadership: This brand of leadership teaches leaders to look for and find the best in people and acknowledge people for the good things they do. It is designed to help facilitate communication between leaders and followers, because the leader actively seeks out input from those below him or her. It makes a working environment friendlier by focusing on the positives instead of the negatives. The central idea behind appreciative leadership and its related field called "appreciative inquiry" is that the leader shows the followers that they are appreciated, and he or she tries to work with their strengths whenever possible in order to inspire passion and build self-confidence among them.

Functional leadership or function-centered leadership: This concept, pioneered by Elisabeth Cox and Cynthia House, means that leadership is function centered rather than person centered.[29] Leadership is viewed as encompassing critical things to be done, rather than as the characteristics of one person. Function-centered leadership requires that all persons practice leadership by leading in those areas where they have critical responsibilities.

Leadership as a process: This brand of leadership makes the distinction between leadership as a solitary act and leadership as a function of the interaction of leaders and followers. Peter Northouse defines leadership as a process during which an individual influences a group of individuals to achieve a common goal.[30] The philosophy behind this brand of leadership views leadership as something that must continually evolve. Leadership is seen as a career or lifelong path. Leadership as a process is a collaborative effort between leaders and followers. It shapes the goals of a group, motivates their behavior towards their attainment of these goals, and defines the culture of the group.

Inclusive leadership: This brand of leadership identifies the fostering of a broad range of interpersonal relationships by the leader as the single most important factor in effective leadership. Inclusive leaders are especially concerned with relationships between them and their followers, customers, investors, suppliers, and the community. They believe that their relationships will lead to sustained growth and development within organizations because they respect their followers and focus on something other than the bottom line. Inclusive leaders act as stewards for their organizations' resources and are willing to share their leadership roles with others. Inclusive leadership views an organization as a network of interpersonal, mutually dependent relationships. Inclusive leaders seek to maximize the potential of the networks. This creates a synergistic effect, because the network, when united in quest of a common goal, produces an even more powerful network. Inclusive leadership is very similar to collaborative, consultative, participatory, and servant leadership in emphasis and practice.

---

[29] Elisabeth Cox and Cynthia House, "Functional Leadership: A Model for the Twenty-First Century" in *Building Leadership Bridges* 2001 (University of Maryland, College Park, MD: International Leadership Association).

[30] Peter Northouse, *Leadership: Theory and Practice: Sage Reflections*, 3rd ed., (Thousand Oaks, CA, 2004).

Proactive leadership: This brand of leadership is based on the belief that leaders look toward the future and make leadership decisions based on their anticipation of two things: what is going to happen in the future, and how their followers are going to react to their ideas, suggestions, decisions, and actions of leadership. This type of leadership requires leaders to understand the future and be able to connect psychologically with their followers. Proactive leaders give feedback and seek 360-degree feedback from those around them. They act decisively and clearly communicate the goals to their followers.

Self-organizing leadership/self-directed teams: Dr. Tomas Hench of the University of Wisconsin, Madison, defines "self-organizing leadership" as "a quality that manifests itself as a relationship between the leader and the led; in the context of a particular challenge, facing a particular group of people, in a particular moment of time." Thus, self-organizing leadership spontaneously manifests itself at any level of an organization in order to meet current challenges. Often, these are communication challenges between and among departments or employees in an organization. Using self-organizing leadership can add significant value to an organization because it helps to capitalize on latent abilities of each member. It also tends to improve work patterns and processes because people concentrate on building their own future and lessens resistance to change, because the people themselves are generating and leading the change.

Category 5
Follower Focus

Collaborative leadership: John Gardner, author of *On Leadership,* defines this brand of leadership as one in which leaders seek the strong input of followers in assisting them in making decisions and leading the group. This brand also requires the followers to join together and offer their time, assets, and commitment to help formulate key decisions that will address the most difficult issues facing a group. According to John Gardner, collaborative leaders inspire commitment and action by creating visions and working with their followers to solve problems. They lead, not from the top down, but as peer problem solvers who help others without autocratically making decisions. They take responsibility for building extensive community and member involvement and for sustaining hope and participation from their followers. They seek input from all involved parties. They help to keep the group on track by setting realistic, concrete goals and by rewarding the attainment of these goals with positive reinforcement. Collaborative leadership looks at the big picture and at long-term goals and considers the global, complex, and systematic nature of problems.

Consultative leadership: This brand of leadership includes building strong relationships and relies on these relationships for organizations to expand and meet challenges. Consultative leadership allows for the strong participation of followers in the decision-making process. It must be flexible and capable of extending across the leadership-followership border, and actually blurring this border. It is designed to deal effectively with problems that neither are clearly defined, nor have obvious solutions. Ron Heifetz refers to these kinds of problems as "adaptive problems."

Empowering leadership: This leadership brand is discussed by Peter Block in his book, *The Empowered Manager* and is very similar to participatory leadership in which the leader delegates authority to followers, empowering them to make decisions, and giving them a direct stake in bringing about change. Theoretically, this reduces the resistance to change and increases the morale of the followers, causing them to work harder, because they are directly involved in leading their organizations.

Entrepreneurial leadership: This brand of leadership instills followers with the confidence to think, behave, and act as entrepreneurs in the interest of their organization. An entrepreneurial leader focuses on encouraging every follower to help create economic value through the deployment of limited resources.

Organizational leadership: This style of leadership, popularized by Theodore White's book *Organizational Man,* stresses allegiance to an organization. It seeks to capitalize on people's desire to be a part of something larger than themselves and urges people to identify themselves as a part of the organization.

Participative leadership: Participative leadership is a type of leadership in which leaders involve others in the decision-making process. Participative leadership is based on the idea that in order to be effective, participative leaders need to encourage their followers to make suggestions and lead the implementation of these suggestions.

Upward/trickle-up leadership/upside-down leadership: Michael Useem, professor at the Wharton School and author of *Leading Up: How to Lead Your Boss So You Both Win,* and Tom Chappell, *Managing Upside Down: Seven Intentions of Value-Centered Leadership,* define upward leadership and trickle-up leadership in which followers are expected to contribute ideas and help make decisions critical to the future of the organization. Leadership, under this definition, originates from the bottom of the corporate pyramid instead of from the higher managerial ranks.

Category 6
Multileader Focus

Distributive leadership: This brand of leadership was made popular by Richard Elmore, professor of educational leadership at Harvard. Distributive leadership stresses the sharing of leadership responsibilities among several people. Distributive leadership is also known as shared leadership, dispersed leadership, fluid leadership, collective leadership, and roving leadership.

Formative leadership: This brand developed by Dr. Ruth Ash and Dr. Maurice Persall from Samford University is based upon the idea that many different leaders should work together within a single organization. Law firms often use this type of leadership through management or executive committees. A formative leader must freely share data, information, and knowledge with a team and also facilitate knowledge transfer within the organization to promote wide distribution of leadership tasks throughout the organization.

Category 7
New Challenges Leadership

Connective leadership: This brand of leadership, made popular by Jean Lipman-Blumen's book, *Connective Leadership: Managing in a Changing World,* takes place when leaders reach across borders (corporate, geographical, and cultural) in order to assist in building communication networks between disparate groups with conflicting needs and goals.

Creative leadership: According to Lyndon Rego from the Center for Creative Leadership, creative leaders seek to create the future in a conscious manner by anticipating and responding creatively to new situations.

Cross-border leadership: This brand of leadership refers to leadership that transcends geographic, cultural, and corporate borders in order to accomplish a given task. It requires excellent communication skills, because the involved parties often have different (if not conflicting) ideas, expectations, and goals. As the world continues to get smaller, or flatter as Thomas Friedman suggests, cross-border leadership will become increasingly important.

Category 8
Nontraditional Organizations

Chaordic leadership: This brand of leadership was popularized by Dee Hock, Founder and CEO Emeritus of Visa International, Inc. He coined the term to describe leadership that is both chaotic and orderly. Chaordic leadership differentiates between the relationship between superiors/subordinates and leaders/followers. The former relationship relies upon the coercive power of the supervisor, whereas the latter is a matter of choice for the follower. Chaordic leadership consists of four behaviors, the first three of which should occupy approximately 95 percent of a leader's time: (1) managing one's own character, (2) managing one's peers, (3) managing one's superiors, and (4) managing those below. In this brand of leadership, Dee Hock defies many ethical leadership theorists by proposing that the duty for ensuring ethical leadership lies within the power of the followers.

Complexity leadership: This brand of leadership, like quantum leadership, draws on the idea that Newtonian physics is not very applicable to the modern business climate, law firms, corporations, or nonprofit organizations. Complexity leadership encourages spontaneous self-organization and unplanned but sensible improvements in the efficacy of organizations. Complexity leaders do not lead from the top down, but rather expect that their followers will form networks and find ways to lead themselves. This means that goals and production strategies are always being streamlined and ensures that new ideas circulate freely in the organization that adopts the principles of complexity leadership.

Consultative leadership: This brand of leadership is based upon the belief that many of today's challenges are bigger and more complex than the abilities of any single leader to solve them. Consultative leaders thus focus on listening, participation, and facilitating a dialogue between themselves and their followers. When this is done properly, it has a synergistic effect for the entire team and creates better solutions than can be created through a command and control or top-down traditional leadership formula. Consultative leadership puts the leader in a role closer to the traditional role of a moderator or facilitator.

Quantum leadership: This brand of leadership borrows its conceptual base from quantum physics and was made popular by Tim Porter-O'Grady's book, *Quantum Leadership: A Textbook of New Leadership.* Although Newtonian physics is dominated by highly structured interactions between objects, quantum theory holds that these interactions are chaotic and unpredictable. Quantum leadership brings this distinction to the world of business and organizational development. Newtonian organizations have the traditional pyramid organizational structure. In Newtonian structures, those on top, the leaders, are expected to control the followers—treating them as tools rather than creative assets. The bureaucratic framework in Newtonian strucutes is rigid and includes multiple layers of approval required when a person at the bottom of the pyramid makes a suggestion for change or attempts in any way to act as a leader. Newtonian organizations find it difficult to adjust their direction, to innovate, experiment, or adapt in the changing world.

A quantum organization, on the other hand, is one in which all members design and manage the organization's systems and processes. Information flows freely from one area of the organization to the other, not just from the top down. Quantum leadership is based on the idea that anyone within an organization can lead and should develop leadership skills. Quantum leaders help people develop self-managing strategies. Ideally, they teach that organizations are as much about growth and development of the individual members or parts as they are about creating products and delivering services.

Category 9
Results Oriented Leadership

Results-based leadership: This brand of leadership was popularized by Dave Ulrich, Jack Zenger, and Norman Smallwood in their book, *Results-Based Leadership.* They explain that results-based leadership places a relentless emphasis on outcomes through the following equation: effective leadership = results. In order to measure a leader's ability or aptitude, one must look to results as the best measure. Results-based leadership focuses on four areas of results: (1) employee results (i.e., productivity), (2) organizational results, (3) customer oriented results, and (4) profits or returns—investor results.

Scientific leadership: This brand of leadership focuses on the ability to measure the effects of leader. The success or failure of a leader who follows the brand or discipline of scientific leadership is determined by how well the people under him or her perform.

Category 10
Leadership Training Brands

Leadership development: This generic category embodies the assumption that leaders are made, not born. Leadership development programs focus on identifying new ways to teach people how to assess and improve their leadership skills. Leadership development courses tend to be based on leadership theories, whereas leadership training is more concerned with fine-tuning technical leadership skills such as speech making, project management, communication, and team-building skills.

Executive development: This aspect or brand of leadership training teaches and develops the skills that high-level managers need. Executive development programs build critical-thinking and decision-making skills necessary to anticipate and meet various challenges.

Leader to leader: This leadership brand asserts that leaders can improve significantly by learning from their peers, other leaders. According to the Leader to Leader Institute, formerly the Drucker Foundation, bringing leaders into a forum with other leaders helps to facilitate communication and idea generation across the public, private, and social sectors.

Leadership training: This leadership concept is similar to leadership development, but focuses on technical aspects of leadership such as project management, public speaking, communication, and team building.

Unnatural leadership: David L. Dotlich and Peter C. Cairo have developed the brand called unnatural leadership, which is learned—hence the name "unnatural." Unnatural leadership promotes the ideas that leaders should think creatively and challenge conventional wisdom, admit when they do not know something and ask their followers for help unnatural leadership embraces the concepts 1) there are many solutions to a given problem; 2) trust others before they earn it; 3) connect with competitors in symbiotic relationships in order to avoid having to recreate the wheel; and 4) be willing to give up some control to improve participation.

Category 11
Situational Leadership

Issue leadership: This brand of leadership occurs when a person takes the initial step of organizing a coalition to oppose or support a given issue. The organizers and leaders of the American Civil Liberties Union (ACLU), the National Association for the Advancement of Colored People (NAACP), the Susan B. Anthony List organization, and other single-issue types of organization fall into this category. In general, issue leaders need to be able to focus deeply on one issue, possess good social skills, and excellent networking skills.

Leading change: This brand or model of leadership promoted by John P. Kotter in his book, *Leading Change and the Society for the Leadership of Change,* focuses on the intention and ability of a leader to create and execute a vision. People who lead change efforts integrate key program goals, priorities, values, and other factors in a dynamic environment where change both occurs often and is necessary in order to address a problem or situation successfully. Leading change requires the ability to balance change and continuity. Kotter has developed an eight-stage model for implementing change: (1) establish a sense of urgency, (2) create a guiding coalition, (3) develop a vision and strategy, (4) communicate the change and vision, (5) empower a broad base of people to act, (6) generate short-term successes, (7) consolidate gains, (8) insure that the changes and new approaches are deeply institutionalized into the culture of the organization or society. Leading change requires leaders to be able to predict and understand when followers, and even co-leaders, will resist change in organizations.

Situational leadership: This popular brand of leadership developed and promoted by Hersey and Blanchard refers to a model of leadership that adopts different styles of leading depending on the needs of the situation and the abilities of the leaders and followers in the situation. Ken Blanchard, author of the *One Minute Manager* series, and Paul Hersey developed the basic model for situational leadership during the 1960s. Situational leadership requires great skill in analyzing a given situation in order to decide which type of leadership style or behavior to use.

Tipping-point leadership: This brand of leadership, first analyzed by Malcolm Gladwell in his book, *Tipping Point,* suggests that in order for leadership behavior to be effective, leaders should exert a concentrated influence on specific areas in order to convince a critical mass of people to adopt an idea or strategy. Tipping-point leaders seek to overcome (1) cognitive hurdles that cause people to resist change, (2) resource hurdles, (3) motivational hurdles, which discourage followers, and (4) political hurdles.

Category 12
Team Orientation Leadership

Synergistic leadership: This brand of leadership is based on the notion of having people and organizations work together to create value from the combined efforts that will be far greater than could be created by each of the parts working independently. This intangible factor results in the 1 + 1 = 3 philosophy of synergistic leadership. Steven Covey has popularized this type of leadership as Habit #6, Synergize.

Team leadership: This brand of leadership differs from traditional top-down leadership in eight major ways. (1) Instead of one person being solely responsible for the success or failure of an objective, the responsibility is shared by a team of people. (2) Final decisions are made by a group of people and not an autocratic leader. (3) Power is decentralized, and the structure of authority is deemphasized. (4) The role of the individual is minimized, or at least deemphasized. (5) Task-oriented functions are performed by the group as a whole and not by single leaders. (6) The team itself is responsible for its self-maintenance. (7) Socio-emotional processes and interpersonal interactions are monitored by team leaders. (8) Expressions of feelings and ideas are encouraged and addressed by the team in open meetings. This leadership model can be inefficient and complicated, as compared with the command and control model of leadership, especially in large organizations. The expected benefits of team leadership include improving morale, increasing the competence and leadership abilities of all members of the team, and capturing the unique abilities of each member for the good of the entire organization. Team building, an essential component of team leadership, is a leadership strategy involving improving team dynamics, clarifying team goals, identifying roadblocks, overcoming obstacles, and facilitating the achievement of the final goals.

Virtual leadership: This brand of leadership is a field pioneered by NetAge CEO Jessica Lipnack, Jeff Stamps, and Lisa Kimball, CEO of Group Jazz, Inc. It asserts that teams with members in different geographical locations that are managed by a manager who is not geographically located with other team members can be very productive, at significantly less cost, than teams in which everyone is located in the same geographical area using face-to-face meetings and communication. This leadership model relies on information technology to foster and keep track of communications, and places an emphasis on creating team unity. Virtual leaders are in charge of designing the projects and holding the team together, which requires considerable communication, usually by phone, e-mail, web conferencing, shared documents websites, and other collaboration software. The May 2004 edition of the *Harvard Business Review* contains a study about virtual leadership and indicates that it can work very well in today's interconnected, globalized world.

Category 13
Traditional Leadership Brands

Coaching or executive coaching: This brand is as old as humans themselves. It is a leadership style in which the leader seeks to help the people he or she coaches find and explore their own goals and capabilities. This type of leadership encourages two-way communication. Ideally, coaching results in the development of the followers and allows them to become more effective as leaders.

Heroic leadership: This brand of leadership is based on the "great man" theory of leadership. Heroic leaders behave as if all the responsibility is on their shoulders and put themselves on a pedestal above their followers. This results in a top-down leadership style that causes followers to become dependent on their leaders.

Institutionalized leadership: This brand of leadership was coined by Elman Service in his 1975 book, *Origins of the State and Civilization: The Process of Cultural Evolution.* Service argues that institutionalized leadership is ingrained both in the legislative foundations of a state and in the functioning of its bureaucratic apparatus. Leadership is therefore fostered by the creation of a detailed institutional framework to allocate decision-making authority.

Military leadership: This brand of leadership refers to leadership that is organized in a top-down fashion. Military leadership is often marked by a rigid hierarchical structure and a well-defined central authority. A clear definition of values and clear lines of authority must exist for this type of powerful command and control leadership to succeed because often what followers do is a direct function of what the leader says they should do. In times of crisis, military leadership can be especially useful. Followers can clearly identify who is in charge and can be comforted and directed by this. By establishing exactly how much and what type of authority leaders in each position exert, everyone in the chain of command knows his or her role. However, this style is subject to lack of accountability, because the authority of the position and the authority of the person can be tied very closely and not easily questioned. Often the military leadership brand does not promote significant two-way, reciprocal communication between the leader and the follower.

Muscular leadership: This is a top-down leadership brand that requires strong direction from the leader and strict obedience by followers. This leadership style contrasts with more collaborative, team-oriented approaches to leadership. David Gergen's article "President Bush's Leadership"[31] and his keynote speech to the International Leadership Association in November 2003 in Seattle, Washington,[32] explain how President Bush uses this brand of leadership.

---

31 David Gergen, "President Bush's Leadership," *Compass: A Journal of Leadership,* Center for Public Leadership, Harvard University (fall 2003).
32 David Gergen, "Perspectives on Leadership" (Keynote speech. International Leadership Association, Seattle, WA, November 2003).

NINETY BRANDS OF LEADERSHIP DEFINED AND EXPLAINED

Operational leadership: This brand of leadership, very close to the definition of "management," focuses on the day-to-day challenges facing an organization. In general, this type of leadership is very different from visionary leadership, which focuses its energy on attaining long-term goals instead of short-term ones.

Powerful leadership: This brand of leadership is espoused by Ruth Sherman in *Get Them to See It Your Way, Right Away: How to Persuade Anyone of Anything*. Powerful leaders are able to retain their influence either by building themselves up in the eyes of their followers or by destroying or eliminating their opposition. It also can result in leadership by fear or resentment, lowering morale, and thereby decreasing productivity.

Rational leadership: According to Marin Clarke, of the General Management Group at the Cranfield School of Management in England, rational leadership gives priority to traditional and accepted processes of influencing people. Rational leaders tend to prefer formal, face-to-face meetings, and leadership roles are very carefully defined.

Transactional leadership: James McGregor Burns popularized this brand of leadership in his book *Leadership,* published in 1976. Transactional leadership motivates followers by appealing to their self-interest. It motivates followers through the exchange process. Modern theorists have added to Burns's model, and today there are four types of behavior that can be considered transactional leadership: (1) contingent reward—rewards are given when expectations are met; (2) passive management by exception—correction and punishment are handed out when performance standards are not reached; (3) active management by exception—leaders actively watch work quality and correct followers; and (4) laissez-faire leadership—leaders adopts a hands-off approach to leading.

Category 14
Visionary Leadership

Level five (5) leadership: Jim Collins developed the concept of *Level 5 leadership* in his book *Good to Great: Why Some Companies Make the Leap…and Others Don't*. Collins identified five levels of leadership. Level 1 leadership is provided by very able individuals whose knowledge, experience, and work ethic enables them to lead. Level 2 introduces the concept of teamwork and synergy, stressing that teams can accomplish more than isolated individuals working on similar projects. Level 3 is the leadership demonstrated by the team leader who motivates and encourages a team to succeed. Level 4 resembles level 3 leadership, but the leader shows more energy and demands more from each team member. Level 5 refers to the leadership given by executives who are personally humble but demand the highest level of performance from their teams. They instill standards and a vision in their followers and use this vision to motivate them. They allow their followers the freedom and responsibility to work together and make their own decisions, while keeping them encouraged and focused on the ultimate goal of the current project. The job of the level 5 leader is to determine how to best maintain high-level organizational objectives, including cash flow and profitability, and help their followers succeed with all key organizational objectives. Level 5 leaders set an example that they expect their followers to emulate. They sacrifice their own egos in order to help their organizations and accept responsibility for poor performance. According to Collins, level 5 leadership is the most important factor in taking a company "from good to great."

Loose-tight leadership: This brand of leadership is explained in Christopher Meyer's book, *Relentless Growth: How Silicon Valley Innovation Strategies Can Work in Your Business*. Loose-tight leadership is a style designed to cultivate new ideas on a regular basis. Meyer claims that it "alternates the creation of space for idea generation and free exploration with a deliberate tightening that selects and tests specific ideas for further investment and development." The first stages of innovation should be "loose," and the innovation process should tighten as it progresses. Too much of either loose or tight thinking can harm growth, because looseness can prevent a company from moving forward in a single direction and tightness can strangle creativity. At the heart of this leadership style is the goal of continuous, rapid innovation.

Principle-centered leadership: This brand of leadership is best captured by an excerpt from Stephen R. Covey's book, *Principle-Centered Leadership*. He writes that "if you focus on principles, you empower everyone who understands those principles to act without constant monitoring, evaluating, correcting, or controlling." Principle-centered leadership thus revolves around a set of principles espoused by the leader and accepted by the followers, who may provide some input to the leader regarding these principles. The leader relies upon these principles as the leader's basis for the decisions the leader makes, the style of leadership the leader uses, and as the basis for leading others in its entirety. The principles of security, guidance, wisdom, and power are often key principles that leaders use to guide organizations that adopt this brand of leadership. Principle-centered leadership is similar to the platform-based organizations discussed in this book.

Revolutionary leadership: This brand of leadership is based on the leaders' and followers' perception that significant change is needed in a given community. Revolutionary leaders are willing to take tremendous risks in order to change present conditions and alter the power relationships that currently exist. A basic problem with revolutionary leaders like Pol Pot and others is they often destroy the historic, traditional way of life and all remnants of it, but do not have a coherent strategy to replace this way of life with a better life.

Strategic leadership: According to Randal Heide, onetime president of the Strategic Leadership Forum, strategic leadership compels everyone in an organization to adopt a shared set of goals and a common vision of how to achieve success. Unlike heroic leaders who use fear or personal charisma to inspire followers or results-based leaders who make decisions based only on the bottom line, strategic leaders allow the principles and goals of the organization to guide their leadership decisions and their style of leadership. Strategic leadership ensures that even though leaders come and go, the guidelines for leadership in the organization will remain constant. Dell, Wal-Mart, and Southwest Airlines are all examples of companies that do business according to carefully conceived strategies. Their success does not depend on a specific leader as much as it depends on a constant focus on strategy.

Visionary leadership: This brand of leadership is directed towards meeting long-term, lofty, significant goals. A visionary leader is motivated by a vision of the future. Visionary leaders often can effectively motivate others to work toward this vision. They create huge, but specific, achievable goals, and their leadership style can contain a balance of wisdom, practicality, and motivation or it can lack an appreciation of how difficult and risky it is to change a currently existing environment.

Category 15
Holistic Follower

Fusion leadership: This brand of leadership has been popularized by Richard L. Daft and Robert H. Lengel in their book, *Fusion Leadership: Unlocking the Subtle Forces That Change People and Organizations.* Fusion leadership brings individuals together in order to accomplish a goal based on common vision and values. Fusion leaders seek to engage the whole person: the bodies, minds, hearts, and souls of their followers. They support personal growth and creative thinking among followers in order to facilitate change. Fusion leadership depends on the belief that organizations function as living things. Part of the goal of fusion leadership is to fuse the organization and the individual followers and leaders of the organization, so that they grow and change together, in similar directions.

Generative leadership: This brand of leadership taught by Drexel Sprecher and others is a type of leadership that does not emphasize influencing other people. Instead, it aims to create an environment in which people continually deepen their understanding of reality, thereby becoming more capable of shaping their own futures. Generative leaders use their abilities to help their followers envision new futures, to articulate them, and, achieve them.

Transformational leadership: James MacGregor Burns is given credit for bringing the concept of transformational leadership to the center stage of leadership study and practice. Peter Northouse's book, *Leadership: Theory and Practice,* defines transformational leadership as a brand of leadership that makes people want to improve themselves and to be led. Successful transformational leaders are able to assess their followers' needs and show them they are valuable. Four factors are included in transformational leadership: (1) Idealized influence—leaders who are trustworthy and are good role models; (2) Inspirational motivation—leaders who can motivate people to commit themselves to the ideals of an organization; (3) Intellectual stimulation—leaders encourage new ideas and critical thinking; and (4) Individual consideration—leaders coach their followers on how to use their strengths and reduce the liabilities of their weaknesses in a constructive way. Transformational leadership emphasizes the needs and strong roles of followers, as well as the reciprocal nature of the leadership/followership relationship.

Category 16
Holistic Leader Focus

Alpha leadership: This brand of leadership, which is distinct from the alpha male brand of leadership, is designed to maximize the effectiveness of leaders while helping them lead more balanced lives. According to Anne Deering, Robert Dilts, and Julian Russell, authors of *Alpha Leadership: Tools for Business Leaders Who Want More from Life,* alpha leadership contains three leadership areas: anticipate, align, and act.

Balanced leadership: This brand of leadership actually has several meanings. It refers to the appropriate balance of numerous personality traits to allow a leader to perform leadership tasks in an integrated manner. Balanced leaders realize that in order to be effective, they must carefully develop and cultivate their mental, emotional, and physical traits in the proper proportions for a given job. Balanced leadership can also refer to a leadership style that is, in actuality, a combination of several different types of leadership. In certain situations a leader may govern one way, whereas in others he or she may use a different method.

Continuous leadership: This brand of leadership builds on the definition of *leadership at every step.* The idea underlying leadership at every step is that leadership is a full-time activity and every action of a leader must be consistent. Continuous leadership expands on this concept and refers to people who are leaders at all times. Continuous leadership involves acting as a role model for one's followers and living what one teaches.

Enlightened leadership: This type of leadership, according to Ed Oakley and Doug Krug, authors of *Enlightened Leadership: Getting to the Heart of Change,* is represented by the efforts of leaders to make the most out of underutilized talent, expertise, and energy within an organization. Enlightened leadership plays a critical role in mobilizing these latent forces. As Stephen Covey mentions, it works from the inside out. Enlightened leaders first become fully cognizant of their own strengths and weaknesses before evaluating others. Enlightened leaders view problems as opportunities for personal growth, both for the followers and for the leader. Enlightened leadership creates an environment of trust and helpfulness, which increases the morale of the followers.

Integral leadership: This brand of leadership has been popularized by Ken Wilber. It requires leaders to combine cognitive understanding and technical knowledge with several types of personal consciousness.

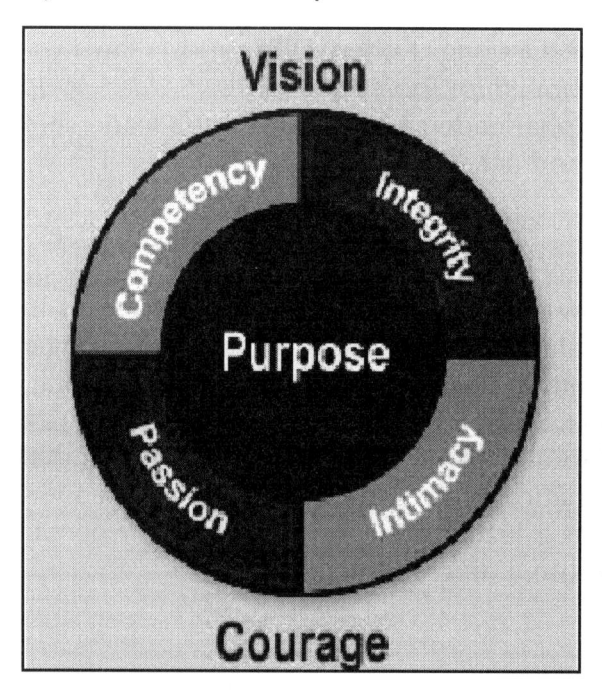

Total leadership: This brand of leadership focuses on team development, personal growth, and 360-degree feedback. Dr. Stephen Payne, leadership strategist and pioneer of the total leadership brand, claims that total leaders both achieve better business results and are more fulfilled in their personal lives. Total leadership is designed to integrate work, personal goals, family, and the community.

Wholehearted leadership: This brand of leadership, developed by Dusty Staub and Staub Leadership Consultants, uses the human heart as a model. Because the heart consists of four chambers, wholehearted leadership consists of four main quadrants: competency, integrity, passion, and intimacy. At the core of wholehearted leadership is a purpose, or goal, and in order to reach this goal, vision and courage are needed. Competency requires being able to understand and deal with the problem at hand and having the commitment to solve it. Integrity involves leading from a moral compass, and indicates that ethics play a vital role in wholehearted leadership. Wholehearted leadership is rooted in strong interpersonal relationships that help to transfer the values of leaders to followers. Passion comes from the leaders' commitment to achieving certain goals and involves the creation of positive working environments. It also demonstrates the leader's commitment to service. Lastly, intimacy is what makes relationships last, and it allows leaders to show that they care about their followers and the community at large. The wholehearted leader's ability to lead successfully is also based on understanding and meeting the needs of their followers.

APPENDIX B
LEADERSHIP EDUCATION FOR LAWYERS: CHALLENGES AND PROMISE

*Speech by Herb Rubenstein, Esquire
To the Annual Conference of the Association for
Continuing Legal Education Administrators
Denver, Colorado
August 2004*

Introduction

The legal profession, and law schools in particular, are currently very resistant to introducing "leadership development education" into law school and CLE curricula. A new course called "Leadership in the Public Sector" has been instituted at Harvard Law School as an elective for law students. My research shows that, with the exception of "Leadership for Lawyers" in Cincinnati and a few other courses, few state bar association have approved CLE courses on "leadership or leadership development" or "leadership theory and practice" for CLE credit in the United States.

I hope to convince you today that leadership education is very important to lawyers, that courses in leadership could be very popular programs for CLE, and that the legal profession could be greatly improved by the creation and dissemination of leadership development courses for lawyers. Ultimately, only good leadership courses and good marketing efforts will determine if there is a strong demand for these courses and if they are useful to lawyers in their everyday lives as professionals.

For Lawyers by Lawyers

I accept from the outset that if a course on leadership is going to be taught to lawyers, it first should be taught by lawyers. Second, it should be based on a rigorous review of the current leadership literature and knowledge base in the field of leadership. Lawyers have a right to demand excellence when a new course is being sold to them, especially one that does not directly meet the ever-growing demand for technical, law-related courses, that help lawyers keep up with the increasingly complex field of law.

Third, any course on leadership should be practical and should be grounded, at least in part, in the tradition of the case method. Because the leadership literature is usually not grounded in the case method, leadership development courses for lawyers need to be developed to use fact patterns that lawyers face with great regularity. Fourth, leadership development courses should include leadership theory, skills development practices, current information, and knowledge, and hands-on leadership practices so that lawyers, in a three- or six-hour format can get a taste of how to improve their own leadership capabilities in an easily digestable format.

The Why behind the Course

Lawyers are called upon to be leaders every day. Sole practitioners who serve on boards of directors, because of their sense of duty and their desire to market their services in an honorable way, often go into these governance situations without proper leadership training. New leaders of large law firms often go to Harvard's M.B.A. program to take a one-week course called "Managing the Professional Service Organization" since there are no adequate courses in this area taught by CLE providers or Bar Associations. And one former president of the D.C. Bar Association, whom I met at the end of his tenure, told me that he certainly could have benefited from a strong leadership development course in his job as bar president.

LEADERSHIP EDUCATION FOR LAWYERS: CHALLENGES AND PROMISE

Today, the legal profession's reputation in the community as a whole is not a source of great pride to the profession. Leadership education could help support lawyers in becoming better leaders, and I believe such a course could help lawyers earn a better reputation in the world at large.

The Course at Harvard Law School

From my recent interview with Professor Phillip Heymann and my review of the Harvard Law School catalogue, I learned the following information about the leadership course for law students at Harvard. The following is directly quoted from the catalogue:

Leadership in the Public Sector
Professor Phillip B. Heymann
3 classroom credits 41790-31 Spring

> Attempting to combine knowledge about personal, organizational, and political relationships through integrating concepts such as "organizational strategy," the course will develop a descriptive and normative picture of the job and responsibility of an elected or an appointed government official. The examples will emphasize lawyers in governmental or political roles. The methodology relies extensively on case studies of people and events, such as: David Kessler addressing smoking at the Food and Drug Administration; Barry McCaffrey as drug czar; Jim Woolsey dealing with spying by Aldrich Ames at the CIA; Governor Hunt and Senator Helms designing political campaigns; or Bill Bratton trying to make-over the N.Y.P.D.
> The object of the course is to increase the sophistication of students about the operations and interaction of government and politics.

Phil Heymann stated that he did not know of any other course on leadership for law students or CLE approved leadership courses and strongly believes that the profession would be well served to begin to have leadership development courses, as required courses for a law degree.

The CLE Leadership Course I Envision

In the first stage of the development of this leadership course, I envision a course that describes the ten leadership theories, describes the ninety-plus current brands of leadership on the market, and identifies and explains the fifty-plus basic leadership behaviors generally accepted as the standards by which leaders successfully operate.

By laying out the ten modern leadership theories, in an evolutionary framework (each latter one builds on the previous one), lawyers and law students taking the course will gain important, practical insights regarding how "leadership" development theory and practice can improve our workplaces, productivity, employee retention, profits, professionalism, decision making, and problem solving and reduce strife inside the law firm and legal organizations.

Leadership development courses should also include a leadership diagnostic instrument that each person taking the course would take to assess their strengths and weaknesses as a leader.

Each person attending the course would receive a confidential leadership "profile" or report, based on the leadership assessment tool. Leadership courses for lawyers should always include a substantial ethics component.

Conclusion

The field of leadership development for the entire legal profession is wide open. It is no accident that Harvard has decided to take the lead in this area with its first course offered in 2003, because the school teaches its students, first and foremost, that they will be the leaders of society in the future.

I think the time is right for such a course to catch fire in the legal profession, especially at the CLE level. I welcome your comments and hopefully your partnership in making this a reality in the very near future.

BIBLIOGRAPHY

American Bar Association, *Annotated Model Rules of Professional Conduct*, 5th ed. (Center for Professional Responsibility, American Bar Association, Chicago, IL 2002)

Bennis, Warren. *On Becoming A Leader.* Perseus Books Group (Cambridge, MA, 2003)

Bennis, Warren and Goldsmith, Joan. *Learning to Lead. A Workbook on Becoming A Leader.* 3rd ed. Basic Books. (Cambridge, MA, 2003)

Blanchard, Kenneth and Johnson, Spencer. *The One Minute Manager.* William Morrow Publishers. (New York, 1982)

Block, Peter. *The Empowered Manager: Positive Political Skills at Work.* Jossey-Bass. (San Francisco, 1987)

Bloom, Michael A. "Lawyers and Alcoholism: Is It Time for a New Approach?" *Temple Law Review* 61(1988): 1409

Burns, James MacGregor. *Leadership.* Harper and Row. (New York, 1978)

Cashman, Kevin. *Leadership From the Inside Out.* Executive Excellence Publishing. (Provo, UT, 1998)

Collins, James. *Good to Great: Why Some Companies Make the Leap…And Others Don't.* HarperCollins. (New York, 2001)

Covey, Stephen. *The Seven Habits of Highly Effective People.* Simon and Schuster. (New York, 1989)

Covey, *Principle Centered Leadership.* Fireside-Simon and Schuster. (New York, 1990)

Cox, Elisabeth and House, Cynthia. "Functional Leadership: A Model for the Twenty-First Century" in *Building Leadership Bridges 2001.* International Leadership Association. (College Park, MD, 2001)

Daicoff, Susan Swaim. *Lawyer Know Thyself: A Psychological Analysis of Personality Strengths and Weaknesses.* American Psychological Association. (Washington, DC, 2004)

Drachman, Virginia G. *Women Lawyers and the Origins of Professional Identity in America: The Letters of the Equity Club, 1887 to 1890.* University of Michigan Press (Ann Arbor, 1993)

Chappell, Tom. *Managing Upside Down: Seven Intentions of Value Centered Leadership.* William Morrow Publishers. (New York, 1999)

Ciulla, Joanne B. *Ethics, The Heart of Leadership.* 2nd ed. Praeger. (New York, 2004)

Ciulla, Joanne B. *The Ethics of Leadership.* Wadsworth Books. (London, 2003)

Clifford, Robert. "Opening Statement: Confronting Our Critics" *Litigation* 28, no. 2 (Winter, 2001): American Bar Association

Daft, Richard L. and Lengel, Robert H. *Fusion Leadership: Unlocking the Subtle Forces That Change People and Organizations.* Barrett Koehler. (San Francisco, 1998)

Deering, Anne, Dilts, Robert, and Russell, Julian. *Alpha Leadership: Tools for Business Leaders Who Want More From Life.* Jossey-Bass. (San Francisco, 2002)

Downs, Larry, "The Killer App." *Harvard Business Review.* December, 2004. (Cambridge, MA)

BIBLIOGRAPHY

Enlightened Power: How Women are Transforming the Practice of Leadership. by Linda Coughlin, Ellen Wingard, Keith Hollihan, eds. Jossey-Bass. (San Francisco, 2005)

Fels, Anna. *Necessary Dreams: Ambition in Changing Women's Lives.* Harvard Business Books. (Boston, 2004)

Fuchs Epstein, Cynthia. *Women in Law.* Basic Books (New York, 1981)

Gardner, John W. *On Leadership.* The Free Press. (New York, 1990)

Gardner, Howard. *Leading Minds: An Anatomy of Leadership.* Harper Collins. (New York, 1995)

Gergen, David. "President Bush's Leadership." *Compass: A Journal of Leader.* Center for Public Leadership. Harvard University. (Cambridge, MA, 2003)

Gergen, David. "Perspectives on Leadership." Keynote Address, International Leadership Association. (Seattle, WA, 2003)

Gladwell, Malcolm. *The Tipping Point: How Little Things Can Make a Great Difference.* Little, Brown and Company. (New York, 2000)

Greenleaf, Robert. *Servant Leadership: A Journey Into the Nature of Legitimate Power of Greatness.* Paulist Press. (Mahwah, NJ, 1977)

Grzelakowski, Moe. *Mother Leads Best: 50 Women Who are Changing the Way Organizations Define Leadership.* Dearborn Trade. (Chicago, 2005)

Harrington, Mona. *Women Lawyers, Rewriting the Rules.* Penguin Group. (New York, 1995)

House, R.J. and Mitchell, T.R. "Path-Goal Theory of Leadership," *Journal of Contemporary Business* 3 (1974): 81-97

Kabacoff, Robert I. *Gender and Leadership in the Corporate Boardroom.* Management Research Group. Portland, ME. www.mrg.com/Publications/articles/APA2000.PDF

Klenke, Karin. *Women and Leadership. A Contextual Perspective.* Springer Publishers. (New York, 1996)

Kotter, John P. *Leading Change.* Harvard Business School Press. (Boston, 1996)

Kouzes, James and Posner, Barry Z. *The Leadership Challenge: How to Get Extraordinary Things Done in Organizations.* 3rd ed. Jossey-Bass. (San Francisco, 2002)

Lavan, Helen. "Dissatisfied Attorneys Have Plenty of Options. Posted at www.careerjournal.com

Linowitz, Sol. M. and Mayer, Martin. *The Betrayed Profession: Lawyering at the End of the Twentieth Century.* Johns Hopkins University Press. (Baltimore, MD, 2000)

Lipman-Blumen, Jean. *The Allure of Toxic Leaders: Why We follow Destructive Bosses.* Oxford University Press. (Oxford, 2004)

Lipman-Blumen, Jean. *Connective Leadership: Managing in a Changing World.* Oxford University Press. (Oxford, 1996)

Ludwig, Arnold M. *King of the Mountain.* University of Kentucky Press. (Lexington, KY, 2004)

Maccoby, Michael. *The Productive Narcissist: The Promise and Peril of Visionary Leaders.* Broadway Books. (New York, 2003)

Meyer, Christopher. *Relentless Growth: How Silicon Valley Innovation Strategies Can Work In Your Business.* Free Press. (New York, 1998)

Morello, Karen Berger. *The Invisible Bar: The Woman Lawyer in America: 1638 to the Present.* Random House (New York, 1986).

BIBLIOGRAPHY

Munsey, Brenda. *Moral Development Moral Education and Kohlberg.* Religion Education Press. (Birmingham, AL, 2004)

Northouse, Peter G. *Leadership Theory and Practice.* 2nd ed. and 3rd ed. Sage Publications. (Thousand Oaks, CA, 2001, 2004)

Oakley, Ed and Krug, Doug. *Enlightened Leadership: Getting to the Heart of Change.* Simon and Schuster. (New York, 1994)

O'Brien, William J. *The Soul of Corporate Leadership: Guidelines for Value-Centered Governance.* Pegasus Books. (Waltham, MA, 1998)

Peskowitz, Miriam. *The Truth Behind the Mommy Wars, Who Decides Who Makes a Good Mother.* Seal Press. (Emeryville, CA, 2005)

Porter O'Grady, Tim. *Quantum Leadership: A Textbook of New Leadership.* Jones and Bartlett Publishers. (Sudbury, MA, 2003)

Rost, Joseph. *Leadership for the 21st Century.* Praeger. (New York, 1991)

Rubenstein, Herb and Grundy, Tony. *Breakthrough, Inc.: High Growth Strategies for Entrepreneurial Organizations.* Prentice Hall/Financial Times. (London, 1999)

Ruderman, Maria and Ohlott, Patricia. *Standing at the Cross Roads: Next Steps for High Achieving Women.* Jossey-Bass. (San Francisco, 2002)

Seligman, Martin E.P., Verkuil, Paul R., and Kang, Terry H. *Why Lawyers are Unhappy.* Cardozo Law Review 23 (2001): 33

Service, Elman. *Origins of the State and Civilization: The Process of Cultural Evolution.* W.W. Norton. (New York, 1975)

Sherman, Ruth. *Get Them to See It Your Way, Right Away: How to Persuade Anyone of Anything.* McGraw Hill. (New York, 2004)

Silvestra, Marissa. *Women In Charge, Policing Gender and Leadership.* Willan. (Devon, UK, 2003)

Staub, Robert E. *The Heart of Leadership: 12 Practices of Courageous Leaders.* Staub Leadership Publishing. (Greensboro, NC, 2002)

Stefancic, Jean and Delgado, Richard, *How Lawyers Lose Their Way: A Profession Fails Its Creative Minds.* Duke University Press. (Durham, NC, 2005)

The Debate: Do men and women have different leadership styles? The Case For By: Susan Vinnicombe, Director of the Centre for Developing women Business Leaders a*nd The Case Against* By: Andrew Kakabadse, Professor of International Management Development. *Management Focus* Issue 12 Summer 1999 Cranfield School of Management, England

Ulrich, Dave, Zenger, Jack and Smallwood, Norman. *Results Based Leadership: How Leaders Build the Business and Improve the Bottom Line.* Harvard Business School Press. (Boston, 1999)

Useem, Michael. *Leading Up: How to Lead Your Boss So You Both Win.* Crown Books. (New York, 2001)

Walters, J. Donald. *Art of Supportive Leadership: A Practical Handbook for People in Positions of Responsibility.* 2nd ed. Crystal Clarity Publishers. (Nevada City, CA, 1987)

Wheatley, Meg. *Leadership and the New Science: Learning About Organizations from an Orderly Universe.* Barrett-Koehler. (San Francisco, 1992)